ALL MY
BURNING
BRIDGES

ALL MY BURNING BRIDGES

Pat Phoenix

Arlington Books
Bury Street St. James's
London

ALL MY BURNING BRIDGES
First published 1974 by
Arlington Books (Publishers) Ltd
38 Bury Street St James's
London SW1

© 1974 *Pat Phoenix*
printed and bound in England by
The Garden City Press Limited
London and Letchworth
ISBN 85140-236-4

Pat Phoenix and the Publishers are grateful
to Gerald Duckworth & Co. Ltd., for
permission to quote from the poem Sanctuary
by Dorothy Parker, which comes from
The Collected Dorothy Parker.

To all my dear ones who
gave me the matches – and
to Alan who gave me a torch.

My land is bare of chattering folk;
The clouds are low along the ridges,
And sweet's the air with curly smoke
From all my burning bridges.

DOROTHY PARKER

Chapter One

I am a bastard. Many people have thought so, and some I am certain have said so, although I hope with a twinkle in their eye. In fact they were right. I am literally a bastard – I was born out of wedlock. Not that my innocent mother, Anna Maria Noonan, accepted it for a minute but she was the unknowing pawn in a game that fate had to play. She loved, lived and laughed with the man who was my father, whom I thought the elf king but who was later to be named by a respected judge, "the chivalrous bigamist". This because although he met and "married" my mother in a registry office he secretly maintained his legal wife for sixteen years.

My father's problem was that he thought all women were lovely and my mother, with her classical colleen features and tumbling rich red hair, certainly was. If a woman asked him for anything he would give it to her, be it help, money or love, and eventually he would find himself in a situation beyond his control. A situation, perhaps, that he longed to relinquish, but on his right shoulder sat the devil who was constantly whispering in his ear and his love for my mother was often outshouted by the whispered titillations.

His name was Tom Manfield. He had Latin good looks. He was quite small although at the time, baby that I was, he seemed a veritable giant. It was said of him many times he had eyes that spoke volumes when they only meant a page. His daughter was later to bear that label. When he laughed the world laughed, but alas, the last laugh was on my mother and finally all she could do was cry.

When I remember what my father did for a living it strikes me that he did everything. He was a part time freelance journalist; he once had a job working with radios for Marconi; sometimes he drove a taxi and sometimes a van. Whatever it was we were never short of money. Our home in Ducie Street, Manchester, is now a run-down area but it was once a street for the grand carriages of wealthy Mancunians. At the time we lived there, we were neither rich nor poor, but happy and comfortable and usually with domestic help.

My father would come in and empty his wallet on the table with total disregard for the notes fluttering everywhere.

"Take what you like," he would say.

"What about you?" she would ask.

"I'll make some more," he'd say. And he did.

He would come home at nine o'clock at night, scoop me out of bed in a blanket and say, "Right, we are all going off to Blackpool."

To a child put to bed at 7.30 this was the middle of the night, the witching hour, and he was a fairy prince come to carry me off – be it only to Blackpool. Be it in a van, taxi or car – to me it was the enchanted coach of Cinderella. Then came a mad round of funfairs where he would spend pounds to win me a one pound doll or a teddy bear.

Life was one long Christmas but the trouble was that he wanted to be Santa Claus to everyone. To this day there are still some of his weaker traits that stuck to me. He was an

exciting and wildly generous man; life was full of laughter
and he never stopped talking. He was a fathomless fund of
very funny anecdotes and if he was not talking we were
laughing so the perpetual problem was trying to get a word
in edgeways. There were always presents, presents and still
more presents for my mother and me.

I was precocious and tiny and he found me a source of
great amusement and for my part I adored him and followed him everywhere. My mother was a fantastic lady full
of fire, guts and spirit and together they were magnificent.
There was great love, great passion, but hand in hand went
Olympus-like tempers. You never knew when Zeus would
hurl a thunderbolt or Diana would shoot an arrow and over
my head across the room would come a maëlstrom of pots,
pans, cups, saucers, knives and forks. Leo, the dog, and I
would run for cover under the nearest table till the storm
subsided. The making-up was magnificent, colourful, tearful and gift-laden.

I can remember those laughter-filled moments when he
piled presents at her feet. They adored each other but he
gave her too many causes to lose her temper and as her
temper was lost his laughter would start like a small, defiant
boy. But always at the height of the storm they would find a
reason for throwing arms about each other and making the
last reel into cinemascope. He was an enchanter; a
magician, a teller of tales. Such tales – and no one could get
a word in.

My mother would laughingly say: "Your father is a
terrible liar."

She had no idea how chillingly true her words were. He
would counter with: "You can't tell your mother the truth
or she just goes up in the air."

My mother was so honest it hurt but she too was a great
romantic in her way and it was her romanticism that led to

the one fib of her life. Manchester, she decided, was a very mundane place for her daughter to be born, and being Irish and having been born in Portumna, County Galway, herself, concluded that it was a more suitable spot for her daughter to have been wished on the world.

The trouble was that years later during Press interviews she stuck to it. When reporters talked to Elsie Tanner's mother she would say, "Oh, yes, she's terribly Irish, you know. She was born in Portumna."

I would wince but a few more million readers would be misled. Once it was in print it was difficult to deny but I would like to set the record straight. I was born in St. Mary's Hospital, Manchester, and it was in Manchester that I spent my childhood. (But if you were to ask me I would *still* say I was Irish and born in Portumna.)

Mine was no easy coming into the world. I took forty-eight hours to arrive and gave my mother pernicious anaemia in the process. But that was only the start.

"She's . . . er . . . different," the doctor said to my mother. I was three at the time, so I don't remember much about it. You must admit that remark can be taken a thousand and one ways and none of them complimentary.

"She's . . . er . . . different" – meaning:

1. She's half-witted
2. Not normal, i.e. sub-normal
3. A raving lunatic
4. Cross-eyed
5. Pointy-eared (I was)
6. Coloured (e.g. red, yellow or blue)
7. A Martian with malicious intent
8. She has fangs
9. She has webbed feet
10. A bastard. (As I was but we weren't to know at the time – mother and me.)

He meant, he translated for my mother, that I was hypersensitive, nervous, aware, too fast, too intelligent for three years old. I would have said too soft, too precocious, but my mother was pridefully satisfied that she had spawned a genius. From this time forward I was treated according to my varying moods as Royalty from the pages of Hans Andersen. (No wonder I have suffered all my life from what a batty Austrian doctor called "The Little Mermaid syndrome") or Lucifer's own, special hell-charged daughter.

My mother would have said, "She was so thoughtful today. So clever! So kind to that kid across the way." Or sometimes

"The devil! The devil! She drank the vinegar, smashed three cups on purpose, swore at me, defied me, refused to go to school. I beat her and she wouldn't cry. She just never cries."

No easy, well-behaved child was this, but a miniature monster set loose upon an unsuspecting world.

It is difficult to know just when or how early I started compensating (or is it apologising) for the creature I was. Anyway, it must have been pretty soon, for I remember my mother's story of how I allowed some stranger to divest me of my baby locket and chain, bracelet and ring, while I sat gleefully gurgling in my pram. I do remember the clout I got for giving away a new tricycle to a completely strange child who admired it. In later life people were to mistake these apologies for myself as great generosity. They still do today.

My crimes were minor, such as using mother's curtains to be the "Woman in White". For that reprimand I threw a tantrum, some purple-faced frothing at the mouth, stamping and even a spit. The blow that followed the spit stayed in my subconscious forever. (When, as an adult, I was required to spit when playing Sadie Thompson in *Rain* I was unable to do it.) I left home a few times, getting as far as the garden gate and threw an unconvincing faint or two for attention; recovering very quickly when I found myself ignored and lying on a very hard floor.

I was the only child of their great love affair. My mother said she took one look at me and that was the finish. Her romanticism reached beyond my illusory birthplace to my christening. She loved, she said, the glamorous, gallant ring of an Irish regiment called Princess Patricia's Own. So when I was born I became Patricia. I am sure she imagined thousands of men marching to death or glory behind their corps of drums, carrying their colours and the name of a woman. To her nothing could be more moving or magnificent. Yet all my life she and others near and dear to me have always called me Tricia or Trish. Never Pat or Patricia. It is not generally known that I sheepishly admit to having the rather grandiose middle-name of Fredrica. Just imagine! Had it been my first name. Fred Phoenix!

My father was mad about cars, motor bikes or anything mechanical. I remember him bringing home a new huge, noisy motor bike which was very fast for its day and he bought them both leather coats to ride it. I would be only about six and I was following him out of the house when my mother told him: "You will not take that child on that infernal machine!"

"I am."

"You're not."

"I am."

He won.

He heaved me on the pillion seat, tucked my arms in his belt and we roared off down Ducie Street at the then reckless speed of thirty miles an hour, and I was flung off on the corner and fell on my head. Some would say that accounts for my characteristical crazy streak but I survived unscathed – which is more than can be said for my father after my mother had finished with him. That was a most terrible row but by no means the most dramatic.

My mother and local help had spent all day long polishing the long tiled hall to a dazzling brilliance. My father, tired after a long day's work, flung himself out of his van, never stopping to wipe his mud-caked boots, tramped up the hall leaving behind him beautiful imprints of size nines all over the floor. My mother, jaw dropped in horror, recovered enough to say scathingly: "We do not spend all day polishing this hall to have you walk up and down it with your filthy boots."

Pause.

Long pause.

"Oh, you don't?"

"No, we don't."

Even longer pause.

"We'll see about that."

Storming out like a Roman about to bring the Christians on to the lions he reappeared one second later carrying before him like a sacrificial chalice, a can of petrol.

A tiny pause.

Then the golden liquid from the can was thrown gently and deliberately over my mother's highly polished floor.

Silence. Nothing but the click clack of my mother's heels as she marched into the kitchen. She returned with a blazing Olympic torch of newspapers. With eyes matching the burning paper she flung it defiantly on to the petrol soaked floor.

A whoosh of sound and the hall was ablaze. My father, innocently child-like, eyes wide with wonderment, said: "Now look what you've done."

Then there was water, soil and blankets to douse the

flames, and laughter and again they were in each other's arms.

I had always believed that my mother's family had some connection with the circus. Apart from a certain aptitude for riding favourite horses and cows bareback round the fields of my grandmother's farm as a child, there was her curious penchant for knife throwing. Her aim and timing were such that she could bury a balanced knife in a door or a tree without really trying.

Early one Christmas Eve, the kitchen full of delicious smells, roaring fire up the chimney, the radio playing the hit song of the moment, "Allelujah, Gonna Shoo Your Blues Away", and small Patricia, hands sticky with raisins and mouth bulging with candied peel, watching the last of the sixpences disappear into the pudding mixture. My father, waxed and polished, putting the final touches to the tiny knot in his tie, announced HE WAS GOING OUT.

From those small beginnings the ensuing row blew round the kitchen like a typhoon. The voices started loudly and got louder. And suddenly my father laughed. A flash of blade before my eyes and a knife stuck quivering in the door a foot from his head.

"Good God, woman, you could have killed me," he shouted.

"I could have done," she said quietly, "but I didn't."

And he left, still laughing. All the days of her life she hated mocking laughter. It is funny, but I'm a bit like that, too.

They were like gunpowder and fire together and my father's laughter always lit the blue touch paper. He usually did as the warning on fireworks instructed, "light the blue touch paper – then retire".

He was worldly in a way yet despite what he did, somehow still innocent. Convention condemned him as a wicked man but he was not. There was nothing wicked about that man. Nothing.

He was working for a Manchester newspaper as Percy Pickles, the promotional personality man who was described in the newspaper. If anyone was quick enough to spot him on his beat – in this case Blackpool promenade – they could approach him and claim a guinea.

With his natty, brown Percy Pickles suit and trilby soaked he arrived home one night and announced that a woman had hit him on the head with her umbrella. My mother asked him what he had been up to and he told her.

"I couldn't get rid of the guinea. It was raining and there was no one on the prom except this woman sitting in a tram shelter looking very sorry for herself. So I said 'Excuse me, Modom (in my best posh voice) do you want to earn a quick guinea?' She acted like a raving lunatic and hit me over the head with her brolly."

My father still looked hurt and a bit bewildered as he explained to us.

I was a terrible child. Self-assertive, appallingly precocious and with a foul temper if my wishes were flouted. I picked up long pretentious words which I dropped quite casually in conversation but with no notion of their definition and usually completely out of context. This was a source of some merriment for father but far from inhibiting me his laughter prompted me to misuse even longer words.

In such a tiny child the gigantic temper was a source of great amusement to my father but my mother tut-tutted her disapproval at his condoning laughter. In childhood, just as now, I was the great escaper into dreams and situations of my own invention. On this particular occasion I was strapped into my high chair. Bored with the food I should have been eating I began drawing patterns on the plate.

The high chair suddenly became a magic rocking chair and as I rocked, tilting it dangerously backwards and forwards, I was escaping into the Arabian nights. I never got there. I was awakened from my dream with a crash as my head hit the fireplace fender. I had rocked just a little too far. There was blood everywhere; the doctor was called and although the gash did not need stitches he swathed my head in bandages.

My mother and father had planned that night to take me to the Manchester Hippodrome as they did once a week, every week. It was the highlight of my young world. Suddenly I was being banished to bed. This, I decided, was not going to happen. Deliberately, and with malice afore-thought, I opened my rosebud mouth, went purple in the face and began to scream. In all the pandemonious hubbub of our house no sound had ever been greater or more piercing. The name of the game was GET YOUR OWN WAY AT ALL COSTS. And I did. My deafened parents felt in no need of conference. Anything, anything to stop the cacophony of sound that was now assailing their ear-drums.

An hour later I was comfortably seated twixt persecuted mother and father, tear-stained but triumphant with my nose resting on the ridge edge of the box bewitched by the magic on the stage. Although I had no means of knowing then it was for me a magic that would never lose its lustre and which would illuminate my life. From the age of six months my parents had taken me to see the shows. There were fifty-two theatres in Manchester and my father had been to every one of them. He loved show business and show business people and I think it is safe to assume he was at least slightly stage-struck.

The most cheerless thing about my early childhood seems to have been my glaring ingratitude. It astonishes me now that my warm, loving, wild and generous parents did not seem to mind.

One Christmas my rudeness was even too much for my father. I awoke to a bedroom full of toys. There were dolls, cuddly animals, a tricycle, stockings and pillowcases packed with presents and downstairs, books and another pile of parcels. My father was leaning against *his* favourite toy, the gramophone, entranced by the "Carolina Moon" that was shining down on him, when I broke his enchantment with: "Are there no *more* presents?"

Stunned. he dropped his favourite Al Jolson record and said: "Well, you cheeky little devil."

There was a celebration every Sunday with my father. In the evening friends and relatives would call and play cards and there was usually a couple of bottles of port and one of sherry on the table. As every child knows the perfect place to play house is under the table, only I never played house under mine. Grandiose from the first, I played castles. There I was with the drawbridge raised and my favourite hound, Leo, at my feet, when a hand, a foolish, unthinking hand, dropped one of sherry and two of port gently to rest outside the castle door.

"Ah, nectar from heaven, or something of the kind. I will sample this goodly gift."

Within ten minutes I became the youngest drunk in history. If not naturally well-behaved, when we had visitors I could always rustle up enough acting ability to kid them I was. But my bewildered father and his card playing company were rudely interrupted by his cheering laughing child under the table. After ignoring warning of what would happen if I did not keep quiet I was ordered out. Once on my feet I tried to skip across the sitting room, staggered, wished everyone present "happy birthday" then slumped into a deep alcoholic sleep.

While parental love and plenty warmed me like a winter coat the frost-bitten fingers of the Depression pointed at Ducie Street. As I ran errands for my mother and aunt I noticed that the smiles of the more prosperous of the local workers gradually gave way to looks that were wary; then worried; then weary. There was a corner bakery which also doubled as a dairy where they ladled the milk from shiny metal urns. As I nibbled the irresistible crusty corners from a loaf I was carrying I noticed, with a start, that the small toffee shop in the street had closed. It was a sign of more terrible times to come.

I was not quite eight when the call came; the knock on the door that would end my life as I had known it. There stood a policeman who said to my mother: "Do the Manfields live here?"

"Yes, why?" she asked.

"Because," he said, "Mr. and Mrs. Manfield are in hospital with injuries following a road accident."

"Oh, no they are not," said my mother. "I am Mrs. Manfield."

In fact it was not the married Mrs. Manfield who was with my father in the accident but yet another woman. His lawful wife who lived miles away read about the accident in the newspaper, traced him and learned of his bigamous marriage to my mother. He was prosecuted but because he conscientiously paid her maintenance for sixteen years, although she had no idea where he was, the court sentenced him to just one day in jail.

My father wanted to stay with us but that was the end as far as my mother was concerned. She cried, never publicly, always alone at night in her pillow but with all her love for him she was too proud to put up with that.

I remember the return of my father, who did not appear to be in the least abject after his experience in the jailhouse.

He parked the car, strode boldly up the street to the delight of the neighbours and the consternation of my mother, seized me and a toy dog firmly under one arm and struck out towards the car. As he was busily stuffing me head first into the car my mother reached me in time to seize my kicking back legs. Then ensued a quite violent tug of war between them with me as the rope in the middle. My mother won, naturally. My father, hardly waiting to follow her indoors, fell on his knees to her. (He really was a very good actor.) In a voice that Garrick or Keen would have envied he pleaded:

"If you refuse me my child at least let me have my record." (This was his favourite, "Climb Upon My Knee, Sonny Boy", for which I am sure he was reading, "Won't you come with me, little girl".) There was another of those dramatic pauses that punctuated their life together. Then came a resounding crash as my mother, with much dramatic gusto, picked up the record and smashed it to tiny pieces on the top of his head.

Not many nights later I awoke to find by my bedside my father with his finger to his lips saying "Ssssshhhhh". He planned to whisk me away. He wrapped me in a blanket and carried me quietly downstairs, but there was my mother blocking the door.

My mother had, with true Irish pride, love or no love, decided to leave the moment she learned he was already married, and leave him she did. At heart she was the rigidly respectable Irish girl. She left the house, she left the furniture and she left penniless. She had nothing except her pride and a small daughter to support. She went to live with friends in another part of Manchester.

Had it all happened years later she might have stayed. That sort of thing might have been happening among society in the twenties but not the working class. It hit them like a hurricane. It struck my mother and that was unjust because there never was a more kind or compassionate woman. Although she was very proper in her own moral behaviour she had never been a woman to point the finger of scorn; she had never turned anything or anyone away from the door. In days when unmarried mothers were objects of scorn and gossip my mother's hand was the one that sought them out and helped them. Her arms were tremendous, she could have taken in the world.

Never once did she admit I was illegitimate because she did not believe me to be so. She knew I had a birth certificate. Somewhere in Somerset House my birth is registered and so was my mother's marriage to my father – sadly, there are two marriage registration certificates relating to Tom Manfield.

To her dying day my mother maintained that I should never say I was a bastard because she was convinced beyond question that I was not. She had my birth certificate and her marriage certificate. To her these were the tangible evidence of the truth – I was legitimate. She told me in later life, "You are not a bastard – so don't say so."

When I told her that the existence of my birth certificate could not change the legal certainty that I am a bastard she hated it. Wherever she is today I apologise for telling this story, but then she always taught me to tell what I believe to be the truth.

When I did realise the truth about my birth it did not really hurt me – in fact it had never hurt me and I can cheerfully say it has never been a chip on my shoulder. Like Shakespeare said, "Now God stand up for bastards!"

Chapter Two

Money was short and my mother, with me to support, was ready to do any kind of respectable work. For a while she was a char, then through my attractive cousin, Deborah, who was a mannequin, she got the chance to join her and model clothes. My mother had the face, the figure and a natural sense of movement and, although very poorly paid by today's top standards, work, perhaps for a week or two, came her way.

She travelled all over the country, mostly modelling Lancashire cotton clothes at exhibitions, cotton fairs, in places such as trade halls and town halls for organisations like the Co-operative Wholesale Society, and she used to take me along. It was in the days of the first cotton slump and all the mannequins would sing a rousing song at the opening of the show to the tune of "Painting the Clouds with Sunshine". I can still remember the first verse. It went:

> The clothes we're showing here
> were made in Lancashire
> We'll soon be painting the clouds
> with sunshine.

When someone wanted children's clothes modelled I would be dressed – usually in little boy's clothes – and put on parade. My dramatic moment came when the lights in one hall failed and I went on and recited "The Owl and the Pussycat" in the darkness. I do not think the audience was rapt but they seemed to enjoy it.

While my mother and Deborah were working I would wander round the exhibitions collecting free gifts and used to come home with tins of cocoa and bars of C.W.S. soap. At the big shows there was always a huge bridal display and I was always a horrible little bridesmaid wearing a cloche hat of pearls and a withering scowl because I never liked being a bridesmaid. To this day I loathe weddings. I was even uncomfortable at my own.

The adult models sometimes showed corsets and cami-knickers which was quite shocking in those days. They had to walk and walk beautifully, in a rather more stylised way than today's fashion. Up and down the catwalk a dozen times or more and it was damned hard work.

Travelling meant that I missed a lot of schooling and at first, staying in hotels and being on the move was exciting. Sometimes there would be a cocktail party after the show and I was just a nuisance in the eyes of the men who were around my mother. She had the most fabulous eyes and she was an abandoned flirt – but that was all she ever did. She had a great sense of humour but was nobody's fool. Men were drawn to her but at the appropriate moment she would produce me and I was always sure she was glad I was there.

I enjoyed the catwalk until I realised what it was all about and then it became boring. I wanted to communicate somehow; I wanted to do something else for the audience; I wanted words to say.

*　　*　　*

Spirited and far more beautiful than I would ever be, my mother did not lack suitors and, although events take longer in fact than they do on reflection, it seemed only a short space of time before my mother accepted a marriage proposal from a man named Richard Pilkington. He was not the romantic millionaire, actor or poet I thought she deserved but a painter and decorator.

One of her main reasons for marrying I am sure was me. She felt that I would benefit from the guidance and the security offered by a suitable stepfather. Some of our friends and relatives had distinct doubts about the match and thought my mother would be happier if she agreed to a reunion with my father, but she would not hear of it.

The marriage took place and we moved to Moss Side, Manchester.

The first seeds of discontent in the new marriage were sown by the worsening Depression and fertilised by my stepfather. The slump swept painters and decorators into bankruptcy, or on to the street corner, and he was among them while my mother continued to make a modest amount of money as a mannequin. Breadwinning brides might be acceptable now but then, in men like Richard Pilkington, they aroused resentment that gradually grew.

To my stepfather, the bread and butter my mother and I earned on the catwalk had a rancid, bitter taste.

To me, there was a vivid contrast between the richness of the fabrics and fashions at the shows and the threadbare furnishings of our new home.

We had no garden and my mother could not live without one. She was from a long line of farmers and was fond of the earth and anything which grew. She went out into the back-yard with a huge crowbar and forced up the flags so that she could lay soil and plant seeds. She had green fingers and plants were quickly persuaded to blossom. In

Stockport at this moment there is a grape-yielding vine which she grew from a grape pip in a plant pot thirty-five years ago. I know, because I once took the trouble to trace it.

Like my mother, I love grass to walk on. I like a tree in the garden and to watch roses coming up big and fast. But also I like the very simple flowers. I have pleaded with three gardeners to plant marguerites. Gardeners are a funny breed. They can be snobbish about the flowers they tend. I think they consider marguerites common flowers but to me they are extremely beautiful and I love them in my garden. This year I met a gardener who for once agrees with me. I now have two clumps growing in my garden.

With my stepfather we moved back to the Ducie Street area where we had spent those delirious, dizzy years with my father.

I enrolled at the same school and at first, totally bewildered, found myself face to face with the crushing cruelty children can inflict on each other – although in my case it was probably prompted by their parents. Everyone seemed to know about our family scandal and the news had seeped through the school – my father was a bad man, a bigamist, and they must not speak to me. I doubt they even knew what a bigamist was.

On my first day back at my old school I eagerly sought out my former "best friend" Marjorie. Running through the crowded playground I spotted her.

"Hello Marjorie," I said, delighted.

Recognition flickered into Majorie's eyes and for a few seconds she stared.

"Don't you remember me? It's Patricia Manfield but now my name is Pilkington."

Majorie's eyes dropped and she shuffled her feet.

"What's the matter?" I pleaded.

Shamefaced, she said: "My mother says I haven't to play with you any more!"

I would much rather that Marjorie had hit me.

What, I wondered, have I done wrong? Why am I being punished?

I could not understand. Others I had played with were silent and would not sit next to me and for what seemed an eternity I was hurt and miserably unhappy before I began to harden and became a rebel.

There was also another reason, equally or perhaps more important why I did tangibly toughen up. That was my stepfather. I had decided he did not like me.

Earlier I had been precocious; suddenly I became outrageous. I decided that the silent schoolchildren would not have the victory and the way to win, I believed, was to make myself an irresistible attraction; a one-kid theatre; a three-ringed circus. I began to invent stories and games, conjuring them out of my fanciful mind. They all wanted tickets for the show.

At home I escaped into a world of books – of fiction and fantasy. I waltzed through the wondrous pages of *The Secret Garden* and held my breath at the exploits of King Arthur. My toys, soft and warm were living things – although they were rarely the regulation little girl's dolls.

I remember one Christmas during the Depression period when I was about seven or eight and money was very short, the whole family, aunts, uncles and cousins clubbed together to buy me the most glorious doll and carriage I had ever seen. The doll was nearly as big as I was and had a beautiful pot face with great eyes, dressed in a purple silk dress, purple velvet coat trimmed with leopard-skin and a leopard-skin hat. It was a beautiful doll in a splendid carriage and I think I owned it for exactly fifteen minutes. I took it outside the front door to show it off. The little girl next door looked goggle-eyed with longing at my new doll.

"You can have it, if you want it," I told her magnanimously.

She wheeled it away, her delight overcoming her disbelief. You don't meet seven-year-old fairy godmothers every day.

I got such a bashing when I got home without my new expensive Christmas present. Beautiful as the doll and carriage were, they had no value for me. I treasured the books with stand-up pictures of castles much more. Not for the world would I have parted with them. The pictures of knights in armour and their fair ladies fired my imaginings, with romances other children were happy to hear. And then we played Round Table games. I remember, I always cast myself as King Arthur, not Guinevere. (Sounds slightly suspect?)

Those children became my audience and I became the little ring master of the organised games.

My mother always sent me off to school spick and span with a clean dress and matching knickers every day; even if she stayed up all night washing and ironing. I can only remember one occasion when there was no clean dress and to my mother's distress and my own dark mutterings I went off to school in the dress and knickers I had worn the day before. I felt most uncomfortable and dreadfully conscious of a small gravy stain down the skirt when a brainwave hit me. I walked into the classroom serene and, to my mind, very smartly attired. The teacher took one look at me and there was uproar.

"Patricia Pilkington," she gasped. "Why are you wearing nothing but your knickers!"

I could not understand what the fuss was all about. I had done the obvious thing and hidden the stained skirt by tucking it into my matching bloomers. I *still* think it was a good idea. To my little friends it was further proof they could expect from me the unexpected.

Because I had decided that my stepfather should be defied I had a degree of defiance of other adults, and in the eyes of other girls that made me a leader. I thought I was Robin Hood – the teachers thought of me as Machiavelli.

My stepfather might have been a fairer man than my memory gives him credit for, but I do know that he could have worked wonders with a little kindness, but to me that was something he never seemed to show.

I do not believe he was a bad man but he was insensitive. I was frightened of all the things children are frightened of, the dark, weird faces and the unknown.

Once in the winter it was dark when I arrived home late from school. I did not know he was in the house. I chucked my satchel over the bannister and started upstairs. Suddenly out of the blackness came a brightly-lit, contorted face, making the most fiendish noises. It was my stepfather with an electric torch under his chin playing, what to him was a game. A game that made him laugh – and brought ter-rorised screams from me. I became completely hysterical and it took my mother half the night to pacify me. To this day I will switch every available light on before I attempt a step in the dark.

I think he resented me as my mother's daughter and not his, but apart from that, he was probably baffled by this sensitive, bewilderingly strong-willed child who showed him both terror and defiance. We had some terrible feuds and he gave me my share of good hidings.

One thrashing I will always remember. It was epic, in cinemascope and colourful. It took place at the top of the stairs. My mother was out. He had a heavy hand and he hit me and hit me – I thought he was going to knock my head through the wall. I can remember resolving not to cry.

"You're not trying hard enough," I spat out. "Surely you can hit harder than that."

And he did. He expected obedience but I could not obey. Not, at least, my stepfather. I was locked in and a thousand and one threats were uttered without effect – except to dig further the deep-rooted resentment we both felt. It was my stepfather who put iron in my soul. To this day I can always be led but never driven.

My mother was always asking me not to upset my "father". But I felt he was completely unfeeling towards me and for a long time I called him "Mr. Pilkington" before I brought myself to call him "father" – for my mother's sake.

A casualty of these constant clashes with my stepfather was my school work. I had sat on my natural father's knee at the age of five and read pulp paperbacks like *Crime Detective*. He had helped me and, quite incredibly for that age, I could read beautifully and everyone was very proud. It was the same at school. I was bright, keen, and the teachers took interest and I tore ahead with my lessons.

But by the time I was nine all that had changed. I had become lazy. I had never been good with figures but I had made some effort. Now my mind closed to them almost completely. My stepfather tried to teach me but all I can recall is his impatience and his raised voice. For me he was a bad teacher and for him I was a worse pupil. I could not see, I could not hear, and certainly could not think clearly. He would shout: "Are you an idiot?"

I would freeze and the figures became a blur. To myself I would say: "No, but for you I will be."

My fear of figures magnified and the maths mistress was a martinet. She knew I was good at English and believed I was being deliberately indifferent. Because of my terror I became worse. She tried to ridicule results out of me and, as I could not bear to appear stupid, I took what seemed to be the only course – truant. I began to concoct stories which would cover my absence on days when there were maths lessons until, of course, I was caught. Which led to another whacking from my stepfather.

Once, I wobbled my way home on my bicycle holding the guilt-ridden evidence of my end of term report. The results were bad enough but the searing indictment of the maths mistress made certain, it seemed, that I was steering my way to hell. I braked and let the envelope go and watched it glide into a puddle. I pedalled like some crazed Kamikaze pilot riding ceremonial circles over the damning document five or six times. When I handed the soaked, mud-stained report over to my stepfather I said: "I'm sorry if you can't read it. I dropped it in the mud."

He shook his head in disgust, anger and disbelief, but said nothing.

I am still paying the price for being a childhood mathematical moron; to this day I cannot count. I cannot do the simplest of sums. I can't play cards. I have to take my shoes off to count beyond ten. But acting needs no faculty for adding. If it did they would never have let me set foot on a stage – even to sweep it – and I think I recognised that when I was very young.

As a child I was as cheerfully stage-struck as the next little girl but at first it seemed that my great and glamorous future lay in the serene, romantic beauty of the ballet. Covent Garden was waiting impatiently to collapse at my feet.

The trouble was they discovered that one of my feet was one and a half inches further away from my head than the other. I had begun ballet lessons but the exercises were agony so I was sent to hospital where the doctors made a simple if staggering diagnosis – my left leg was longer than my right. There was a quick exchange between my mother and the doctors.

"Well," she asked. "What do we do about it."

"We will," a doctor decided, "operate."

He went on to explain, "It should be fairly straightforward but your daughter will probably always walk with a limp and she must for a while wear calipers."

"To hell with that," my mother told him. "She will stay as she is even if she never dances."

And that was that. They did not operate and I did not dance, not even to this day.

They warned my mother that I would probably pay for her decision in later life and in effect I have, but I believe it was the right one. She could not bear the idea of me walking with a limp and, compared to that, not being able to dance is a very small price to pay. I could have been quite the lame duck.

My mother took me to see specialists and they recommended different exercises but when I tried them I fell over and soon got fed up. As a child it took time to accept I had something like two left feet and that I would never dance but, before that really dawned on me, I had decided it might be even more fun to dedicate myself to a dazzling future on the stage.

Had I been a little boy, I would probably about that time have changed my plans to become a pirate to a future as a fighter pilot. So Pat Pilkington, the budding ballerina, became the aspiring actress. A desire to be a nurse should have come next, but somehow that never came.

I got my bottom smacked for one of my first performances. I was nine years old and had organised an impromptu children's concert in our backyard. My mother came home to find me in her black chiffon dress with nothing on underneath doing a snake dance. I can remember the curtain coming down very quickly and, after a paddling, I was put to bed. But I suspect my mother was secretly relieved that her daughter of the one short leg was obviously not letting it worry her.

Ballroom dancing has always been impossible. Once around the floor and I am in pain with my spine but I became quite good at faking modern style dancing of the stand still and wiggle sort. I shake my shoulders just as I did in my mother's chiffon dress and my arms and hands are going like mad but my feet do not move. Always I suffer the slight inconvenience of an aching back and leg but never, as a child or young actress, did I see it for one second as a hurdle or a detriment, although later during the course of my sometimes chaotic career it has agonisingly announced itself.

Elsie Tanner in *Coronation Street* stuck her hip out in a saucy way which was very much Elsie but, in fact, it was very much me. It was right for the character but also the easiest, laziest way for me to stand. Elsie had developed a mannerism that some people found appealing and all because of my short leg. My most excruciating moment came while I was appearing as Annie Sullivan in the stage play *The Miracle Worker*. It was a fight scene and I had to fling a fellow actress around when suddenly there was a click, which I was certain they could hear at the back of the circle.

For a second I thought I would have to call for the curtain to come down. There was a pause and faces appeared wide-eyed in the wings.

They had no idea what had happened, but I had; it was my blessed back. The pain eased a little and I carried on, but I saw a quick succession of osteopaths after that. They all said the same: "You ought to have a built up boot," and suggested exercises.

I still have a one-and-a-half-inch lift one of them recommended that I should wear in my shoe, but it lies in the bottom of a drawer and I never wear it. Weeks after my back cracked on stage I was still not right and I felt it would have to click back before the pain cleared. I was stepping down some stairs from a stage door where some of the audience were waiting for autographs. Suddenly it snapped back and I emitted a great roar of relief. They looked bewildered but probably assumed that I always behaved in that manner when I came off a stage or that I possibly had had one or two in my dressing room. I defy anyone, to this day, whether I am stark naked or fully dressed to notice that I have a missing one-and-a-half inches.

Not present at my stuck-to-the-spot snake dance was a little boy who nevertheless was charmed by my mere appearance. His name was Kevin O'Malley, who declared his love with the sweet shyness of a nine-year-old and saved to buy me a large bar of chocolate for my birthday. My first suitor! The trouble was, Kevin, who lived a couple of streets away, was younger than I was. He was nine and I, by then, was ten and I knew that was not quite the natural age order of romance. He would call for me and we walked to school together and one of our romantic rituals was exchanging comics.

My favourite poet at that time was Omar Khayyam and I am sure I used to bore the poor lad stiff by reciting great chunks to him. Kevin became a teacher and then a priest, but we saw each other only three or four times in the long intervening years. The last time I heard his voice was over the telephone in November, 1972, when I was the subject of *This Is Your Life*. I was stunned and delighted when they said that Father Kevin O'Mahoney was calling from an

African mountain mission in Ethiopia. He reminded me of the chocolate, the comics and the Rubaiyat. Mickey-taking friends who knew about Kevin have often reminded me since, that after a flirtation with Phoenix one lad was so shaken, he took to the priesthood. It's utter rubbish, but it raises a laugh.

My tenth year was the year of my first tender conquest but it was not, in terms of affection, so successful for my mother. Her second marriage had started to slide. Fights between them were frequent and the making-up more strained. Finally my stepfather took to staying out, and again I would awake to the sound of my mother trying to silence her sobs.

I remember creeping downstairs to find her gazing through the window watching the dawn rise while my stepfather was still out carousing. Her face was tear-stained and I can still feel her hand on my shoulder as she said: "Don't ever get married – it's not worth the unhappiness."

She was not to know at that time those words – spoken in a moment of pain – were to remain stamped on my heart and mind for the rest of my life.

My second great uncertainty was born at that moment – a deep distrust of men. I have known many men in my time, acquaintances, friends, and a few have managed to overcome my distrust and suspicions simply by being super nice guys and becoming intimate and true friends. As for the rest, believe it or not and I know you won't, they frighten me to bloody death!

No matter how bad I was at maths, I cannot, come to think of it, have been too bad at English. Mind you, such talent as I had I have managed to lose in the intervening years, but my former English and drama mistress, a super little lady called Dorothy Manley, appeared, much to my surprise, thirty years later on television when I was the subject of *This Is Your Life*. Had she considered me completely unsalvageable, I doubt if she would have consented to come.

I was eleven when my childhood way with words resulted in a sudden radio broadcast which signposted the way destiny would drive me. I had written (or overwritten) an idiot monologue on the death of Lady Jane Grey which popped, more in hope than anticipation, into the postbox, addressed to the BBC in Manchester.

I was impressed when they wrote a very adult reply inviting me to the Studio to record a reading of my monologue, but I have no idea what age they thought I was. Wide-eyed and wondering I went and read it for them and got myself a job on BBC *Children's Hour*, which was a nice periodic thing spanning some years.

I had changed schools and it was at Fallowfield Central School for Girls that I came under the care and encouragement of Miss Manley. (I might also add the school was also known as the Church of the Holy Innocents – What! Me?) I was cast as Tintageles in a school play – me, a boy prince of all things. One thing is for certain, I couldn't do it today without an amputation. The play was called *The Death of Tintageles* and Miss Manley's comment – allowing quite a margin for her kindness – puts me in my scholastic place at that time.

"Pat was not exactly a model pupil (understatement if you like!) but at the same time, on stage, she was just marvellous and I shall never forget her performance as Tintageles." Nice thought. (I might add I have given many performances since that would be best forgotten.)

But in my early uncertain steps on to a stage, someone believed in me.

Twenty-four years later I worked with the girl who had played my sister in *The Death of Tintageles*. Dressed in gorgeous mediaeval clothes made up out of old velvet curtains, she played the Princess to my Prince. It was Betty Alberge, who later played Florrie Lindley in *Coronation Street*.

My stepfather and I stayed, in spirit, poles apart while poverty took a step nearer and, for the first time, my mother had to make the humiliating trek to a pawnshop. Although I was unaware why she was doing it and I still do not know what she pawned, the trip to the pawnbrokers was prompted by me.

Whit weekend was a few days away and that was the traditional time for those girls whose parents could afford it to parade in new dresses. In the past my mother had always somehow managed it but the real gravity of the situation did not strike me even when I heard her utter adamantly, "She will have a new dress. If it is the last thing I do she will have a new dress."

And I did. Whit Monday saw me pirouetting prettily in it but I had no idea of the price she had paid for it until much, much later.

Chapter Three

For the rest of my school life, which lasted until I was eighteen, I continued to be a thorn in my stepfather's side. He would make some sweeping statement at home and I would check what he had said at school and prove him wrong – which drove him potty.

I read books and absorbed print like blotting paper, racing through them so fast he did not believe I had read them.

"You haven't read that already," he would say.

"I have."

Then he would take the book, turn the pages and question me about it. I would delight in going into detail, which would make him hopping mad. He demanded obedience and met with stubbornness and for me, sometimes the bitterness burned my mouth.

One way and another my years as a teenager were hell. I was almost insanely sensitive, particularly if I was with someone rather nice, and would wait for hours rather than say I wanted to go to the loo. I would suffer agonies rather than ask where the toilet was while my stepfather's humour was lavatorial, and I found it shocking. To me, his comments were crude and ugly and they made me cringe. Life was hurtful and hateful and I have tried to erase the most prickly memories completely. Although I cannot say my mother had married beneath her there was no doubt in my mind that she had married a man of far lower intelligence.

My unhappiness too was also a question of my uneasy conscience. I was, in my own eyes, guilty either wilfully or unwittingly of certain chilling childhood crimes. The first was that my mother had a very hard time during my birth. She had collapsed from anaemia after leaving the hospital because she had given too much to get me.

Secondly, if my arrival was a disaster, my very existence made the matter worse. Had I not been there they could have spent more time alone together and their marriage might have stood a better chance. I felt that but for me, they might have had children of their own. Lastly, try as I might, there seemed to be no means of communication with my stepfather. To him I was a walking source of despair and disillusion and perhaps jealousy.

The climax of our constant clashes came in the kitchen on a day which stands clear in my mind – which is not surprising as the occurrence could have resulted in me spending many years behind bars for manslaughter.

I was seventeen and my mother had just a few days earlier been discharged from hospital following an operation for duodenal ulcers. A row erupted between her and my stepfather. They were raising the roof and, although I had said nothing, I thought he was being unreasonable. Then he raised his hand to hit her. There was a carving knife lying on the kitchen cabinet, I grabbed it and held the point pressed against his stomach. He was terrified and went ashen with fright. I was bursting with anger and strange elation as I watched the knife tip touching his belly.

My mother shouted, "Stop, stop, stop." I put down the knife and said, "You're not worth it but don't ever touch my mother." He did not say a word and it was over.

Since then, I have always been very wary about really losing my temper and I rarely do – only when too many straws have been heaped upon the camel's back. When I do flip I usually find that I have done something outrageous and there is no going back or making amends, so I try constantly to avoid it.

The insensitivity of my stepfather always made me shudder. When I was in my teens there was an older and quite wealthy man who was interested in me. I did not give the situation a second's serious thought, but my stepfather knew the man and of his interest. He said, referring to the chance of me going to bed with the man: "Oh well, you're old enough and nobody will miss a slice off a cut loaf."

I was, as it happens, a virgin at the time.

I was at that time anti-marriage. I would say: "I'm not going to get married. I shall go on the stage and live my life in hotels, but I suppose I shall have boy-friends."

Despite her own experiences, my mother would throw me one of her looks of definite disapproval for mentioning boy-friends without marriage but later, when we talked about children and I did not express any urgent need to have them, she said: "Oh well, if you have none to make you laugh, you've none to make you cry." It was a sound piece of simple philosophy but I accepted it as a reflection of the sadness my birth had brought her.

Later, after I had left home and was living for a while in London, my stepfather and I became more reconciled. He decorated my London flat for me on one occasion and I went out with him for an evening. I think he was either trying to make amends or no longer saw me as a threat.

He began to accept me for what I was and I remember,

with some slight affection, one really good laugh we had together over two large spiders called Claude and Cecil which kept appearing in my London flat but which I could not bring myself to kill. He understood then why I could not kill the spiders, I hate killing anything, but earlier he would have thought I was being stubborn. We laughed at the silliness of the spider situation and also with pleasure at what was a small step towards a new understanding.

Chapter Four

Except for the occasional fleeting glances, I did not see my real father until I was about thirty years old. I was appearing in repertory theatre in Bramhall, Cheshire, and one of the theatre staff tapped on the dressing room door and said: "There's a gentleman at the stage door who says he is your uncle and would like to see you."

"Another suitor," remarked some wag.

Puzzled, I went out and there was my father, standing awkwardly, fingering one of his inevitable stiff collars with his tie knotted as tightly as ever, but looking no older than when I last saw him. I was flabbergasted, he seemed just the same. Then he told me about his marriage to a lady named Lucy and of his two sons.

He had, he said, kept track of me and had come to see the show. He and Lucy had built up a happy, respectable life and business together – they had a florists and greengrocers shop and a large house in Walkden, Manchester. They had worked side by side and had done extremely well, and I don't doubt that his charm helped to build up the business while his humour and wit kept the customers entertained. He should have had a slogan: "It's fun to buy flowers from Manfield."

We saw each other spasmodically and I later met Lucy, who was a quiet, sweet, charming woman – although my existence, I feel, must have been an irritation to her. He eventually came home and met my mother again and, once again, there was great laughter and he insisted that if my mother had been "more tolerant" things would have been different.

More tolerant, I ask you?

He did not seem at all surprised at me becoming an actress.

"Aye," he said. "You were born like that. I knew you'd be something!"

Later, when I was cast in *Coronation Street*, he came to see me again and asked me to make a personal appearance for him. He was involved in a function which the mayor and local dignitaries would attend. I told him – yes. On the day of the event we were climbing the steps in front of the hall where everyone was assembled when he turned to me quickly and said: "Don't let them know I'm your dad – say I'm your Uncle Tom. I've got to think of Lucy and the boys."

I was stunned. I knew what he meant all right but it didn't make me feel any better. It felt like double desertion. Once at eight years old, and now again. I was never to be allowed to call anyone father. What he had not realised was that under what appeared to be a very self-assured lady was a little girl he had left at the age of eight, who wanted back what could never be brought back.

Lucy knew I was his daughter, but his sons did not. It was to save embarrassment, he said.

I withdrew from him but we would still meet two or three times a year. My mother was living with me and I can remember him making the point that although he had visited, I had never invited Lucy to the house.

"Why should I ask Lucy," I asked. "She is a nice woman but she means nothing to me."

Also, my mother had not met her and, although she bore Lucy no ill feeling, she did not want to.

My father, who smoked Woodbines all his life, died of lung cancer at the age of seventy-two, saying that he was too young to die. And he was.

His funeral was in Walkden, Manchester, but my mother could not bring herself to go. I went.

A good number of relatives were there and a lot of his friends, including the Mayor, councillors and Corporation officials. By the graveside I put a bouquet on the pile of wreaths and attached to it was a note on which I wrote:

> We'll go no more a roaming
> In the stillness of the night
> Though the heart be still as loving
> And the moon be still as bright.

I addressed it to "My Dear Father, Tom. With love from Pat Phoenix."

The note caught the eye of one of my father's councillor friends. There was a terrible silence, then he said: "Was Tom your father?"

"Yes," I said, and walked away.

I don't apologise for that. It was the one time he couldn't deny me.

Chapter Five

When I was nineteen or thereabouts I was invited to what turned out to be a very special party. Perhaps the most special of my life.

"This is Bill Nadin," said some anonymous soul. No bells rang, no rockets went off, no poetry sounded in my ears. And yet all of those things *should* have happened. For this young man was in a way my destiny. He worked in an engineering plant and we began to go steady. Every morning he would ride past my house on his way to work on a bicycle, whistling "Rhapsody in Blue" to wake me up. I only have to hear the tune today to think of Bill. Ours was a very romantic affair. At nineteen, and a very young nineteen, I believed passionately in knights in shining armour. Bill to me was such a knight. He was Heathcliff to my Cathy; "whatever our souls are made of his and mine are the same".

Bill in turn put me on a pedestal, like someone very special, very rare. All my life he treated me like a child. Even today he would take a box of matches from my hand in case I should burn my fingers.

At nineteen there was a volcano building up inside

me – passion, curiosity, what have you. I knew nothing of men. I was an only child with no brothers or sisters, sheltered and with no contact with the opposite sex whatsoever. Sex struck unexpectedly and accidentally. Bill, thinking I was experienced in the way of the world, discovered to his consternation that I was a pure, unsullied virgin.

Such a gentleman is he that I am sure we would never have become lovers had he known. His first reaction was to marry me right away but my mother, being the woman she was, wise and sensible, avowed we were both too young and in my case I think perhaps she was right. No man alive could have lived up to my youthful dreams and we were soon to part. I demanded total fidelity, thought, word and deed. Knights in armour did not go chasing after other fairy princesses. But it seemed my knight had done just that. Because of a misunderstanding I had mistakingly believed him to be unfaithful. In truth he was not but I was gone before he could deny it. I went out of his life forever. Or so I thought.

One night, many years later in Piccadilly, Manchester, I hailed a taxi. The driver pulled up and I, with total disbelief, heard him say: "I've been waiting sixteen years for this moment."

It was Bill Nadin. We just took up where we left off.

Not long after our meeting came *Coronation Street* and the whole wild whirligig began. Pat Phoenix was in demand – to open shops, supermarkets, factories, council flats, in fact anything that had a door on it. Without Bill I could not have coped. He became my road manager. For a while he continued to run his taxi business. He would don chauffeur's hat and drive me in one of his taxis to whatever function we were attending. Invariably I would be met by a dignitary who would assist me from the car and instruct my "chauffeur" to park round the block. Bill would drive off and return a few minutes later minus his chauffeurs' hat, whereupon I would introduce him to one and all as "my business manager". It always gave us a laugh. As things progressed Bill began to devote more and more time to my affairs and it seemed sensible to give up the taxi business.

Bill is one of the most masculine of men I think I have ever met and yet I could telephone from the studios to home and ask him to pack an evening dress ready for a personal appearance that night with all the trimmings and he never let me down. He would turn up at the studios with not only the right bag and shoes to match the dress, but the right bra, all the right underwear and suitable pieces of jewellery. He could do all this without losing one jot of his masculinity.

I don't know how I would have managed without him on personal appearances. He was always there at my side protecting me from too much jostling and rescuing me from too-long queues for autographs. (He did this by joining the queue himself and snatching the pen from my hand when he reached me and hustling me off before the public got a chance to see what was happening.) It was always: "She's lovely, but what a nasty fellow she had with her."

Darling Bill doing his duty and playing the heavy where I could not. It was always Bill who shepherded me about and drove me to and from wherever I wanted to go. It was not only crowds he protected me from, but from all the harsh realities of life. If someone put a leaflet about animal cruelty through the letter box he would destroy it before I could see it and get upset. There was a sort of conspiracy between he and my mother. "Don't tell Pat. She'll only get upset," was their watchword.

Some of our funniest, happiest moments together were with Bill at the wheel and me sitting beside him. I remember once we were driving down the motorway and a car full of youngsters kept in turn overtaking us, dropping behind, driving alongside and generally riding round us in circles. This was nothing new. It sometimes happened if I was recognised by passing motorists, particularly kids. This lot were making a proper nuisance of themselves. Bill was just getting really furious when the car buzzed alongside us, the windows were wound down, and four famous faces appeared.

"Yoo hoo, Elsie," they screamed. "Elsie Tanner!"

It was the Beatles. John, Paul, George and Ringo doing their cheeky best to send me up. I stuck my tongue out at their grinning faces and was rewarded with a big cheer.

It was not only the happiest moments for Bill and I that happened in cars, but some of our biggest rows. I very well remember coming back from Cornwall on a very hot day and we were going hammer and tongs about something or other. While I nattered on, Bill, one hand on the wheel, took the top from a yoghurt carton with his teeth and took an angry swig. It had soured. With a grimace he threw it out of the window. Unfortunately, the window wasn't open. The carton flew back and its smelly contents showered all over us. Bill swerved to a stop and turned to face me, yoghurt dripping from his eyebrows, his eyelashes and in his hair. I took one look at him and collapsed in hysterics. I've only got to say sour yoghurt to Bill today to bring tears to his eyes.

We took many happy holidays together. Often to Yugoslavia, a favourite of mine where I can scrounge around in a bikini, no make-up, get brown as a berry and go fishing with the local fisherman. The first time we decided to go to Yugoslavia we had no clear idea of where to go.

"Let's pick out a place with a pin," I said. Bill, indulging his idiot child as usual, let me go ahead. I prodded haphazardly at the map. It could have been a disaster, I suppose. Instead it was heaven. The place I picked was Sveti Stevan, a favourite haunt of President Tito I later learned. It is, without a doubt, a jewel of a place.

We visited many of the surrounding villages and in most, there being no English television in Yugoslavia, I went around unrecognised. Except in one particular village where I was sure, and so was Bill, that people were pointing me out to each other and whispering excitedly.

"They don't get *Coronation Street* here, do they?" I worried Bill.

"Of course not," he said stoutly.

We walked on and the whispers and polite pointing increased.

"They *don't* get it here, do they?" I whispered again.

"No, you daft ha'porth," insisted Bill, a little less certainly.

Then we walked into a little shop. From behind the counter came a fat and black-dressed jolly Yugoslav woman who chattered excitedly and threw her arms around me. I was puzzled out of my mind. She seemed to sense it and said what I understood to mean that surely I was the lady of the cinema. I did my best to explain that I was on television, in England. She rummaged behind the counter and came up with a dog-eared film star magazine which she produced, excitedly pointing to a coloured picture of . . . Well, if I hadn't known it wasn't, I would have said Pat Phoenix. My doppel-ganger, I finally understood, was a famous Yugoslav film star who had been born in the village. We were fantastically alike and I am not surprised the whole village had thought I was she. I would have loved to have met her face to face.

I once owned a house in Cornwall where Bill and I, my cousin Ivy and her husband, cousin Cyril, spent many a happy holiday. Bill and Cyril would go off fishing and I would drag Ivy off for long windswept walks along the beach. Most of the time she came uncomplainingly enough. But one day when I had walked her for miles looking for shells along the shore, I turned round to call to her and found her lying full length flat out in a pool of water. The tide had been swirling in swiftly, caught her ankles as she stepped into a hollow and brought her to the ground face down. She was fully dressed for a November walk along the shore. Coat, hat, gloves, boots – the lot! Waterlogged.

"Ivy, what are you doing down there?" I asked.

"I fell, you silly bugger," was the terse reply.

After that I had the greatest difficulty in persuading Ivy on shoreline hikes.

For over ten years Bill and I jogged along together. We had our ups and downs like any couple, but I think we were happy for most of the time. I certainly was, anyway. I am not sure exactly when we began to grow apart. I know that I would come home from the studio worn out and wanting nothing more than my own fireside and Bill would want to go out on the town. He was happy to go out to the pub with his mates and we seemed to spend less and less time together. We got to the stage where we were not communicating any more. Our lives seemed somehow to separate. When I worked late at the studios I would stay in Manchester and Bill would be at home in our Cheshire house. I stayed more and more in Manchester and we saw less and less of each other. When my mother died we became closer for a while but it *was* only for a while. By then we had drifted inexorably apart. Then Alan Browning came into my life and there was no room for anyone else. I think Bill was jealous then for a moment. He and Alan could hardly have been described as the best of friends. But finally things worked out. Bill married and Alan was best man at his wedding. Bill returned the compliment when Alan and I married. Bill now runs The Navigation; the pub of which I am the licensee.

He gave me eleven years of his life and for that I am always grateful. I will always love him. I think somewhere, someone made a mistake in the universe because Bill and I ought really to have been brother and sister. We are inextricably bound together. Lovers once, and today – loving friends.

Chapter Six

School over, I worked briefly in a library before making my mark at Manchester Town Hall Gas Department, a mark that took them years to erase. For some bewildering reason I worked in the accounts department where they totalled the gas bills and sent them to the customers. It was a nice respectable job, but letting me loose among accounts and a mystical addressograph system was an act little short of lunacy. I was going berserk and the addressograph system had me beaten. I caused unwitting chaos by putting the cards in the wrong place and upside down and the gas bills were going to the wrong homes with the addresses printed upside down. I was told that it took them years to get the system right again.

I would have been completely baffled by that kind of work at the best of times but my spare time stage activities made matters worse. For one thing I was often late, and life seemed to be a running race with the round, reproachful face of the clocking-in machine. I was already a member of the Manchester Shakespearean Society run by Derek Joseph (whose leading man was a marvellous old actor called Norman Partridge) when it amalgamated with the semi-professional Manchester Arts Theatre.

For them I played *Major Barbara*, Jessica in *The Merchant of Venice* and, among other roles, Desdemona in *Othello*. But Desdemona on stage in the evening was frequently upstaged by that damned clocking-in machine at 9 a.m. the following morning.

A kindred spirit who worked in the Town Hall was Freddy Bracegirdle. Freddy, who played in a dance band in the evenings, had precisely the same problems as myself with the tell-tale clock. We would meet in front of it, both breathless, inevitably a few minutes late.

One morning, late again, we raced towards the clock. It was the second time that week and it was serious so Freddy produced a brainwave. I had to "faint" on the spot, he would run into the office hollering, "She's fainted, she's fainted". In the ensuing chaos the fact that we were a few minutes late would be forgotten and, if not, we would swear that we were in front of the clock on time when I collapsed.

I did a stage swoon and Freddy fled inside to cause confusion. The whole office ran out and collected in a concerned circle. As I lay with my eyes closed, there were cries of "give her air", and "get some water". Then one randy gentleman who must remain nameless said "her blouse is too tight", and knelt down and began to undo the buttons. Eyelids fluttering frantically, I "recovered" with surprising rapidity and gave him a very old-fashioned look.

There must be more to life than the Town Hall and the addressograph system, I decided, and gave in my notice.

Encouraged by my love of the sea and anything to do with boats I opted for a life on the ocean wave and sent off for the forms to join the WRENS. I had the necessary qualifications and was sure they would accept me. My mother and Bill were dismayed. They were sure I would not survive away from home and their supervision. They put their heads together.

"No," they told me firmly.

My mother refused to sign the form giving her permission and Bill said: "If you want to do war work *I'll* find you some."

Although the war was over, everyone was obliged to do National Service for two years after and while I had been exempt in the Town Hall, I was now a red-hot candidate for an aircraft factory. Bill got me a job at Fords Aviation at Trafford Park. To me it was like entering the gates of hell. I was hypersensitive in the literal sense and to walk into this room, filled with clanging machinery and smelling of a mixture of oil and water, was purgatory. Every woman in the place had her head shrouded in a navy blue snood – a safety precaution to stop stray hair becoming entangled in the machinery.

I endured it for six months and finally terminated my engagement with a long and severe illness brought about by strain. When I was better I still had war work to complete so I was seconded to a small factory specialising in radio components.

My only solace was the stage. I was still with the Manchester Arts Theatre and enjoying huge success playing Judith in *Granite*. It seems I lit up the stage – or so they told me. Derek Joseph felt he had a sure-fire hit on his hands. If only I could get out of war work he would take the company on the road. A full professional tour. I *must* at all costs get out of that factory.

Chapter Seven

Beautiful Lesley Ward gave the performance of her long and distinguished career for the benefit of rows of goggle-eyed girls on a factory bench and the intransigent manager of the radio factory who was standing in the way of me and the stage.

"I will get you out of there, deah!" she had promised. "You shall be removed!"

"You can't! You can't. It's war work," I had protested.

I will never forget the afternoon she swept into the factory, swathed in furs, exquisitely made-up and trailing clouds of perfume. I froze in the monotonous act of slotting one bit of radio to another and waited for the wrath which would surely descend on my head once the unsuspecting manager discovered she was there to spring me from my factory prison.

Looking and sounding every inch the leading lady Lesley launched into a tirade on my behalf.

"You! Fellow!" she called. "Are you the manager chappie?"

The manager hurried forward, all obsequiousness in the face of such a vision.

In a voice which never had any trouble reaching the back row of the stalls she proclaimed: "My deah man, you are wrecking this talented child's career. You cannot keep her in a place like this. You are depriving the English stage of its most promising hope for the future." (An overstatement if ever there was one!)

There was plenty more in this vein and by the time her wonderfully imperious performance was over my fellow workers were regarding me with awe and the manager was promising my immediate release. He was probably as tired of the mess I was making with his radios as I was bored with putting them together. As Lesley picked her elegant way over the radio pieces that littered the floor, supported on one arm by the now completely bedazzled manager, she dropped a wicked eyelid at me and murmured, "It's on!"

And "on" it was. Off we went, a motley band of six, headed by Derek Joseph, packed into an old four-seater car with scenery strapped to the roof and toting a trailer bulging with props and costumes.

Up and down the country we went, playing army bases, airfields, hospitals, old people's homes, village halls; anywhere they would pay to see a play. We were never certain of our wages nor where we would sleep that night. Sometimes we slept in the nearest barn and at one village local farmers paid us in chickens, cauliflowers and cabbages.

There were no stage-hands, front of house house managers or ticket office ladies. Instead, we stuck up our own hand-bills, put up the scenery, sold tickets at the door, then rushed backstage to change into our costumes ready for curtain up.

I was enjoying great success playing the tragic Judith in *Granite* and revelling in my first full professional engagement. I was too young to care that the costume I wore at night was often damp because the trailer tarpaulin leaked and we sometimes had to pool our pennies for petrol so our little old car could lurch on to the next stop. The car began to feel the strain. A slow puncture developed and Derek would make us all get out and take twenty turns each at the footpump while he stood by coughing consumptively and urging us to greater effort. The car nearly killed us in the end.

Four of us were, as usual, crushed uncomfortably together on the back seat on our way to the next date. We had been on the road for a couple of hours and my head was beginning to ache. Derek, luxuriating in the front seat next to the driver, was used to bitter complaints from the back.

"Derek, there's an awful smell in the back and it is giving me a headache," I said.

"You should have got used to the smell of actors by now," he quipped. "It's just your imagination," he added. "I can't smell a thing." He opposed on principle any suggestion of stops along the way and had a cavalier disregard for our comfort.

Fifteen minutes later I tried again.

"Derek, I feel funny," I said, my voice slurred.

He turned in his seat.

"Well, you all *look* pretty funny, too," he said, determined not to be taken in. By then the four of us were slumped against each other, upright only by virtue of the fact there was no room to fall down.

"All right," sighed Derek. "As a reward for a first rate performance of playing dead you can all stretch your legs for ten minutes round the next corner."

No one stirred. Derek leaned across to shake me and my head lolled forward. Alarmed, he shouted: "Stop the car!"

He and the driver flung open the doors and hauled us out on to the grass verge where, coughing and retching, the fresh air revived us.

Apart from being thoroughly sick, none of us were any the worse for our dose of carbon monoxide poisoning.

They were happy, hilarious days but more than that I was beginning to learn my craft. People are nice enough today to complement me on the way I sit, stand and move about a stage. For that I thank Lesley Ward who taught me so many of the tricks. It may look easy to sit down on a sofa centre stage in a full short dress and keep the colour of your drawers a secret from the front row of the stalls but like so many things, it's not as easy as it looks.

Because of my one short leg it is more comfortable for me to slouch with my knees apart; a stance ideal for Elsie Tanner but not tantamount to convincing the sceptical in my *Coronation Street* days that I was capable of classical roles. Scepticism drives me wild, particularly the sneering sort. Once a stranger to the *Coronation Street* fold – a visiting director given a week's try out, implied rather nastily that we all began and ended with the characters we were playing – particularly me. I flipped.

"Listen, cock," I growled, hands straddling my spread knees. "I've probably forgotten more about this business than you have yet learned – and what's more I am still learning – which is more than can be said for you – who apparently know it all."

I am happy to say he never came back to the *Street*. But may I say these occasions were rare. Most of the time I had a healthy respect for the majority of experienced directors, like lovely June Wyndham-Davies, June Howson and Pauline Shaw. I did lean a little more towards the ladies, I suppose. To me they showed more sensitivity and looked further beneath the surface. Not that I didn't see great talent among the males – Bob Hurd, Quentin Lawrence and many others too numerous to mention – I was just prejudiced towards the ladies.

Once, soon after leaving the *Street*, I was chatting with a couple of young actors who were boasting of their days with the National Theatre. They were being a little patronising and I felt it was time to throw a little cold water.

"Oh, yeah, the National," I drawled. "I turned 'em down."

They spun on me incredulous eyes.

"Yes," I said. "I was invited to play in *Mother Courage*." And so I was, but I was doing something else at the time. I had forgotten all about it until that moment.

After that they ceased trying to impress me. To actors the National Theatre is a sort of Valhalla, an ultimate goal. Actors seldom talk about the National, especially those who have never been there, without somewhere in the next sentence murmuring the word prestige.

But unfortunately I did not learn my job at the National – I learned it at fit-up – which is what theatricals call a touring company like the Manchester Arts. I learned how to handle an audience, how to hold their interest, how to behave, how to assess them, because every audience is a different one, and most important, I learned what to do when things went wrong. It was a training that was to stand me in good stead all my life.

Judith, the tortured heroine of *Granite*, was a strenuous part, very turbulent and I thought at the time (thank God, times change) very much me; a part I don't think I would have the energy to tackle today. Every scene was a climax. Its dramatic momentum depended much on the audience's wrapt attention.

I remember once playing an RAF air base at St. Helen's. The *Granite* set was dwarfed by the vast aircraft hangar where we were performing. The front rows were filled by officers in armchairs and the ranks sat in serried rows on wooden benches stretching back as far as I could see. The play was going well when I launched into Judith's speech on which the play pivoted.

"Oh, God, I've sat here ten years," – I emoted, "between stone walls, beside a stone man . . ."

I was interrupted by . . .

Plonk, plonk, plonk . . .

I could hardly believe my ears. One of the officers in the front row was steadily banging his pipe on the arm of his chair and completely ruining the atmosphere of tension I had so carefully built up. I froze in mid-sentence and directed an icy stare at the absent-minded officer.

The audience moved uneasily. I remained stock still centre stage gazing down icily. An urgent nudge from the culprit's neighbour.

"Eh!" said the officer.

"She means you. It's you she's looking at!"

"Eh! What! Oh! Sorry old girl!" he said loudly, gazing up appealingly at my frosty face, dousing the offending pipe, and I continued – to his and the audience's relief. That incident taught me a very valuable lesson; how to handle audience interruption and turn it to advantage.

Judith was a great part and although I was really much too young for it I took myself and the theatre very seriously in those days and I believed I played it well. As a matter of fact I thought I was God's gift to the profession! I don't know now whether I was marvellous or terrible in the part (I have a slight suspicion I might have been pretty lousy) but I think I got through it on sheer energy and vitality. To my surprise people still come up to me today and say: "I shall never forget you in *Granite* when you were Pat Pilkington." That of course, could mean anything!

Fit-up taught me to cope with the unforeseen. One night we took the play to a large, isolated hospital where iron gates clanged shut behind us and we were locked in our dressing rooms until it was time to go on stage. I was right in the middle of a tense scene with Derek, who was unfortunately playing a character called Joseph. At the mention of the name a voice boomed out: "Joseph. Son of God!"

There was a wild thrashing sound from the audience and I looked at Derek in mystified horror, certain we were getting the bird at last.

I struggled through the scene somehow and when we came off stage rounded on Derek and demanded to know what was going on.

"Well," he hedged. "I thought it best not to mention to you that we were playing a lunatic asylum."

Then there was the night when one of the actors threw me off the stage into the orchestra pit. It was not, I hasten to add, deliberate. The stage was highly polished and he had drunk rather more than was wise. Seizing me by the arm he delivered the impassioned line: "Oh, Judith, why can't you leave the girl alone!"

His move was to push me gently away from him but instead he sent me crashing. I managed to scramble back on stage, for all the world like an all-in wrestler, skirts round my waist, in time to say my next line. The show must go on – or so we are told – at all costs. Through bruises, torn skirts, I continued to talk. This ability has come in useful more than once down the years.

Once in the early days of *Coronation Street* when a tight schedule had left us short of time, I was filming a scene with Annie Walker. It was a lengthy dialogue and, racing the clock as we were, we both dreaded a mistake or a slip which would mean valuable time lost in re-shooting. It was going perfectly and we were seconds from the end when there was an almighty crash. The set where we were filming was cheek by jowl with the set of the corner shop which that week, for some reason, was piled high with tins.

The camera operator had backed right into the tiered cans and sent them toppling. The noise was deafening. For one frozen minute Annie and I looked at each other then, quick as a flash, I said: "I'll kill that flamin'cat!"

Some cat! It was more like a herd of elephants. Upstairs in the control room the then producer, Jack Rosenthal, swallowed hard – and grinned: "Bless her! Bless her!"

Chris Sandford and I had a literally very fiery scene once in *Coronation Street*. As Dennis's friend, Walter Potts, he was supposed to be talking to Mrs. Tanner in the kitchen of her home. During the discussion a frying pan was meant to catch alight and the dialogue to continue while Chris doused the flames. Instead of a few flames, the whole pan went up with a whoosh. Chris finished up by putting it on the table and standing on it. It was hilarious but we both managed to stick to the dialogue and save the scene.

I had a scene with Bill Roache, who as the *Street's* school-teacher Kenneth Barlow, is always the one to make social comment. It was all about decimalisation, a new and complicated subject back in the days of pounds, shillings and pence. With my non-aptitude for figures, I could not understand one word of what it was supposed to be about. I assumed Bill understood it, though. We had done a couple of rehearsals and as we were going for the take I said to Bill: "It sounds like a load of old cock to me. I'm glad *you* know what you're talking about."

"I haven't got the faintest idea," confessed Bill.

We played the scene grinning our heads off.

"That was a wonderfully natural way to play it," commented the director, pleased.

Granite gave me other opportunities to exercise a talent for improvisation. We arrived at the theatre late one evening and I hurried into costume and took my position on stage. The scenery was hastily put up around me. The curtain rose and we began to play the scene. I was not required to move from position until I reached the line: "I can dance! I can dance, Prosper! I can dance like Lady Hamilton!"

Whereupon I would take a graceful turn around the stairs and at the end of the scene run up some stairs with a great flounce. By some unlucky chance they had nailed my dress under the scenery and I could not move an inch. I gave a determined wrench and the whole of the back panel of the dress came gracefully away almost in slow motion, leaving me, underdressed as usual, in suspender belt and panties. From that day I have always worn the correct underwear for the costume – corsets, bloomers, petticoats – the lot! I played the rest of the scene without turning my back on the audience and my graceful dance that night was more of a side-step. As for flouncing up the staircase – well, never did a leading lady back off upstairs so beautifully.

I was young for my years and, despite my very warm friendship with young Bill Nadin the year previously, I was still the soul of innocence. The leading man was, to say the least, slightly obsessed with me and disinclined to take "no" for an answer. He kept up the relentless pursuit throughout the tour, hell bent on getting me into his bed.

We were playing at a small town near the Malvern Hills and after the show a young reporter came back-stage to meet the cast. I found him a kindred spirit. Irish, like my mother, a talker like my father and every bit as fey as I was myself. We wandered off together, too deep in conversation to notice the scowls of my rejected leading man. He said he knew of a fairy ring on top of the Malvern Hills and together we would find it and make a wish. Believe it or not, I took it for gospel. It was all my romantic soul could want. We climbed the hills in the moonlight, two souls in unison and searched until the dew was on the grass. We found the fairy ring and I don't remember what I wished but it was all totally romantic and utterly, utterly innocent. We laughed and sang together and I don't think he even kissed me. Well! That's my story and I'm sticking to it. But it was nearly dawn when I arrived back at the hostel where the cast were spending the night.

It was an old-fashioned place with rooms leading off one long corridor. I crept along the corridor determined not to disturb anyone. Suddenly before me stood a figure. It was my leading man, frothing with rage and jealousy, convinced I had given to another all that I had denied him – and all that jazz.

"You whore! You harlot!" he screamed.

"Let me past," I said. "You're crazy. Just go away."

I pushed past him into my room and before I realised it he was behind me.

"What you can do for others you can do for me," he threatened.

I tried to push him off but he was propelling me towards the bed.

"Oh, for Pete's sake, calm down," I said. "You'll wake the whole house."

But he was too far gone. He threw me on to the bed and as I tried to rise his hands went round my throat. I wondered idly what I looked like with a purple face. He started banging my head against the wall. My breathing became more difficult as his grip on my throat tightened and I felt this was carrying the drama too far. The bangings of my head on the wall got louder.

"What an idiot," I thought. "If he's trying to kill me he's not doing it very well."

Suddenly the lights flared and the whole company was crowding into my little room.

The noise of my thick head against the wall had woken

them. It had also woken the landlady who followed close behind in dressing gown, curlers and outraged respectability, demanding to know what was going on in her house.

It was Derek Joseph who suavely saved the day.

"Madam," he placated. "I'm terribly sorry we disturbed you. We're having an early morning rehearsal, you know. The murder scene from our new play. How shocking of us to make such a noise. Do forgive us."

Such was his charm the landlady, casting doubtful looks at where I sat choking and blue on the bed, allowed herself to be propelled from the room.

"Now, where were we," he said in resonant tones as she retreated down the corridor. "Page 38 . . . from the top, everybody please . . ."

Chapter Eight

After eighteen months on the road with the Manchester Arts Theatre I was ready to spread my wings. James Lovell and Arthur Spreckley were running a thriving repertory company at Chorlton-cum-Hardy and with a few days off from the tour I had gone to see the show. Arthur Spreckley spotted me in the audience.

"You're the girl who played in *Granite* aren't you?" he asked.

I was pleased and flattered he had noticed me and even more so when he asked me to play *Granite* for them as soon as my tour ended. It was just for a week but when it was over I was invited to join the company full time. The thought of learning a new play each week was daunting (learning lines has never been my forte) but somehow it all came easier than I imagined. I played a couple of comedies, a welcome relief from the unrelieved gloom of *Granite*, and developed a liking for them. Arthur Spreckley advised me to stick to heavy drama.

"You're hopeless in comedy," he told me. Of course, from that moment on I was defiantly determined to play comedy.

But it was Geoffrey Kellett who was my undoing at Chorlton – literally. We were playing a comedy called *It's A Boy*. Wardrobe is always a problem in weekly rep but I had managed to borrow a very smart black moire taffeta dress from a splendid lady called Mrs. Mullings, wife of opera singer Frank Mullings. With a little matching black hat perched on my head I felt every inch the smart sophisticate.

Came the scene I had to take Geoffrey in a caveman style embrace, positions reversed as it were. I leaned over him, took him in my arms and released him. He was to slide slowly down my body to the floor.

Ghastly tearing noise.

A look of consternation on Geoffrey's face as he gazed up at me.

A button of his jacket had caught in the top of the black dress and ripped it from neck to hem.

I stood once again revealed in brassiere and panties to the accompaniment of uproarious laughter from the audience.

We gagged through the rest of the scene, me clutching the torn black dress as best I could around me. My mind in a whirl. What on earth would I tell Mrs. Mullings? In fact, somebody told her for me. We were still on stage when she came into the theatre and was told: "Pat Pilkington has just torn her dress from neck to hem in the kiss scene."

"Yes," said Mrs. Mullings fatalistically. "And I can guess which dress it was, too."

In spite of that disaster Mrs. Mullings later became my agent and always my very dear friend and was later to be instrumental in getting me my break – and changing my life.

Geoffrey and I were spotted by the movie moguls at Chorlton Rep and invited to make a film. It was not quite Hollywood – Dickenson Road, Manchester, actually.

John E. Blakely had been making pictures in a small way since silent days. He began in the industry at his father's two hundred seat cinema in Warrington, Lancashire, and worked his way up to owning his own film company – the Mancunian Film Corporation. He has the distinction of starring George Formby in one of his pictures when he was still an unknown Lancashire comic. If his pictures weren't winning Oscars they were hugely popular with the public.

Blakely had just moved from London and a rented studio behind Euston Station to Manchester and his own studio. It was actually an old disused church complete with pulpit, pews and organ but with its massive, high ceiling it made an adequate film studio. Before long the trappings of prayer were tossed out and we moved in to film *Cup Tie Honeymoon*. It was a comedy and I played Sandy Powell's wife. We could not then have conceived that some twenty years later it would be shown to millions on television, not once but twice. First, when Sandy Powell, whom I adore, appeared on the television programme *This Is Your Life* when I was a surprise guest and a year later when I myself was the subject and Sandy the guest.

It was a glorious hot summer when we made the picture. One of the scenes took place in a fish and chip shop so somebody went out and bought about a ton of fish and chips from a local chip shop. But unfortunately the scene took much longer to shoot than was anticipated. Instead of taking half a day we were still at it three days later; and we were using the same fish and chips. The temperature in the studio was high and by the time the scene was in the can there were some very pale and green looking actors around the set. I think the scene was eventually rushed through because no one could stand the smell of the fish and chips any longer.

Filming over I returned to Chorlton rep to find a new boy had been taken on. He was a local lad. Occasionally he played small parts but his big chance came when they asked him to play the front legs of a pantomime cow. He upset a lot of people by coming down to take his call at the end of the show minus the head.

"I don't care," he said. "They were going to see who played that cow if it killed me."

He was very good at carrying sofas on his back up the fire escape to the second floor. It was marvellous training for the role that made him famous – as Steptoe's son. I often wonder when I watch Harry H. Corbett on television now if he ever looks back on those Chorlton days.

My few weeks as a film star(?) sent my stock soaring at Chorlton but unfortunately it generated some resentment among a few of the cast. I began to get leading roles others thought, maybe rightly, I was not ready for. Life became a little uncomfortable. I have never been one for back-biting or backstage bitchiness and I felt it was time to move on.

Chapter Nine

The next three years saw the beginning of a life-long love affair. From first sight the Bronte country took my heart and my imagination and never let go. To Keighley I went, along with Geoffrey Kellett, to the West Riding of Yorkshire to join the Lawrence Williamson Players at the Hippodrome.

The role chosen for me was Catherine Earnshaw in *Wuthering Heights*. I can neither understand nor explain with what passion Catherine dominated my life. I was not just playing Catherine – I *was* Catherine, or so I thought. She took possession of my mind and entered my soul. I began to wander the moors by day discovering their stark, barren beauty and listening for Heathcliff in the whistling wind. One day I met an old man up on the hills with a kind and knowing face who sat with me on an old stone wall and told me stories of the moors. I listened enthralled. Suddenly he turned sharply and asked: "Thee must be an actress from yon theayter in't town."

"Yes," I told him breathlessly. "Have you been to the show."

He shook his head.

"Nay. I don't go to nowt like that."

A bit crestfallen I wondered in that case why he should have thought I was on the stage. His answer was even more deflating.

"Nobbut an actress would come up 'ere with sandals and red muck on her toenails."

I was steeped in Bronte and became firm friends with the curator of the museum at Howarth Parsonage, home of the Bronte family. I believe he was called Mitchell but I always thought of him as "Mr. Howarth". He used to take me for long walks over the moors, thick with mud on grey winter days, and together we would discover the old boundary stones of the parish. There was a time when I knew them all.

I still go back to the Silent Inn at Stanbury, near Howarth, and find a solace no other place on earth can provide. I went back recently, with my husband, Alan, my cousin Ivy and dear friend, Harry Littlewood. It was a spur of the moment decision as we sat around the fire at home in Sunny Place Cottage one afternoon.

"Come on. Let's go to the Silent Inn," I said.

When I awoke the next morning I leaned out of the windows where the open moorland melted away in the distance. The air was sharp as crystal, a cockerel was crowing and from far away a faint sheep's "baaaa" echoed. The bells of Howarth began to ring. If life has peaks of perfect happiness then that morning for me was an Everest. Some day I would like to own a pub up on the moors with a barn theatre attached.

My years at Keighley were happy and fulfilling. I played all the magnificent leads for the grand sum of £7.50 a week – and that was big money in those days. Nevertheless one could only afford one meal a day. The kindness of people I shall never forget. Like the baker who sent us cakes and the butcher who sent us meat. We were always being invited out to teas and suppers because the public who loved us thought we were all half-starved; rightly so. We shopped at the second-hand shop for our clothes; the grand evening dresses, the riding breeches, we wore on stage. With the money we were earning you could not pay digs, buy ten cigarettes and afford to eat regularly as well. The warmth of the Keighley people has stayed with me to this day. I made many friends there and I never forget them and 1 don't think they forget me.

Chapter Ten

Keighley went out in a most beautiful conflagration – the stage covered in flowers, audience and cast alike weeping. We didn't want to go and the public wanted us to stay. It was a sad parting. I moved on to Bramhall, Cheshire, for a short time where one of my leading men was Ronnie Barker. I remember giving him a fourpenny one on stage. I was playing Mariella in *The Shining Hour* and he was playing the son of the house. I had to slap him in the script but that particular night I really walloped him. And all because he went a little too far in the stage kiss. And both of us in nappies at the time!

It was there I met Glen Melvyn and his wife, Joan, who became friends of long standing. Glen had the most marvellous sense of humour and I laughed more at that time of my life than I had ever done before or since. Glen taught me to laugh at myself, for which I shall always be grateful. After a few months at Bramhall came a telegram from Harold G. Roberts – "Come and be my leading lady at Halifax".

I went there to meet H.G.R., Charles Simon and a handsome, polite young actor named Peter Marsh.

I had not been long at Halifax when Charles Simon asked me to join a company he was forming as an actor/ manager, once a common combination. They were marvellous some of those old actor/managers. Charmers all of them. They knew how to bleed your heart and get the best out of you. Charles Denville was such a one. I worked with him at Northwich. I vividly remember one week when takings were low and Charlie was wringing his hands and bemoaning the fate of managers.

"There's not one of you would say 'I'll go without my wages this week, Charlie'," he cried dramatically.

"*I* will," I said, ever swift to don Lincoln Green. He took it, too! Damn him!

Working with people like that one learned something about the business. Charlie was a legend. He had a marvellous face and head and, but for his stature, he was very small, he might have been the Lord Olivier of his day. He was a great drinker, too, which in no way affected his dramatic ability except that he tended to go into the wrong play occasionally. It was very disconcerting to be half way through scene one of *Shop At Sly Corner* and find Charlie had just thrown you a line from *No Room At The Inn*, which you weren't due to do until next week.

He also had a habit of wandering into rehearsals on Thursday and taking a sudden dislike to the set of a play due to open next week. He would want all the windows and doors altered around so that entrances carefully learned would have to be unlearned and a new lot memorised by Monday. As soon as he had gone out again we would put everything back where it was, trusting that by the next time he saw the set he would have forgotten all about the changes. He usually had.

Actors who worked for him would dread Christmas and

what was known as "Charlie's glitter call". As soon as the
curtain came down on Saturday night, out he would come
with glue pots and brush in one hand, bags of glitter in the
other. The cast, still in make-up and costume, would be
given directions. Down would come the palace set, or
whatever, and up would go the cave scenery ready for the
pantomime.

"Right, leading man," Charlie would say, spreading his
glue indiscriminately over the cardboard rocks, "you can
have the pink and green glitter. Give leading lady the silver
and gold." And all the while he daubed glue around he
would be muttering: "We've got Mrs. Lesley's Lovely
Babes, too. (Child Dancers.) Little buggers! She wants
fifteen bob for 'em this year!" And he would have the lot of
us decorating the scenery with glitter and making flowers
for the village green scene – and all for a pantomime due to
open on Monday. As I said, they knew how to get the best
out of you.

Charles Simon was one of the best of the latter day
actor/managers. A superb professional. His voice became
familiar to millions as he was Dr. Dale on BBC Radio's
Mrs. Dale's Diary; a part he played for many years. When
he asked me to join the new company he was forming at
West Hartlepool I was delighted to accept. Peter Marsh,
the good-looking young man from the Halifax company,
came along too.

At West Hartlepool most of the company were packed
into the same digs – as is very often the case in rep. It's
more fun that way – drinks after the show, post-mortems
round the fire, who didn't say what line, creeping in late,
shoes in hand so as not to disturb the landlady, Sunday
afternoon walks and Sunday evening pictures. Young,
dreaming – all of us. Tomorrow's hopefuls.

One Sunday I didn't feel like going to the pictures. It was a fine windy evening for a walk on the beach. Peter shyly offered to be my escort. As I got to know him better I found him not only charming, but keenly intelligent, with much more depth than I had suspected beneath that handsome face. Weeks sped by and it slowly began to penetrate my thick skull that he was interested in me in a way that was more than friendly. I have always been slow to see other people's affection for me. In fact, throughout my life, I have always been the last to know when someone cared deeply for me. The whole world could be beaming approval – but me – I live on another planet.

So, I was to say the least, surprised to find myself clutched (deliciously) in a more than warm embrace. Well, that's how it started.

We were beautifully happy for two years – with me as usual pushing thoughts of marriage as far away as possible. Finally parental influences intervened. There was pressure from both sides for us to become respectably married. We gave in.

Bradford Cathedral has never seen such a day. The bride, dressed as though for execution in a pale blue Mary Tudor outfit, followed down the aisle by juvenile girl, Jean Kitson, as bridesmaid and two kilted pageboys, one urgently wanted to wee. The bride could be heard muttering darkly about "all this and two performances tonight is too much to ask of any mortal". The whole of the Northern theatrical scene turned out in full force and the provost had to make a speech to the audience (sorry, congregation) asking them to please remember that this was a church and not to stand on the seats.

There was no honeymoon. That night we were back on stage playing in *The Devil and the Deep Blue Sea*. "When you are between the Devil and the deep blue sea, the deep blue sea looks very inviting," goes the quotation. How true! The marriage lasted a turbulent twelve months but it was nine years before we finally got around to getting a divorce.

The blame for the break-up can be equally apportioned, six of one and half-a-dozen of the other. If we had not been under parental pressure, both from his parents and mine, we probably would not have married at all but remained, as the papers say, "just good friends".

In spite of the fact that I was twenty-six and Peter younger when we married, we were still too young, too young in the head. Out of the two of us Peter was the worldly one. I *looked* sophisticated and wasn't, he *looked* innocent and wasn't. Today, Peter is no longer an actor but a successful advertising man. The only legacy left of our union is that people sometimes ask him, "Is it true you were married to . . ."

Just before I married Peter an older actress said to me: "How many affairs have you had?"

"Two," I told her.

"You should have one hundred and two by now," she said.

I disagreed with her then and I would now. For me, sex should be with someone you love – not just another encounter to send up the score. My love life has never been of the casual kind. I have been deeply loved in my time. Maybe my trouble was that I was always too busy to give my love life its full value. Meaning that my job came only too often before the happiness of my fellah. Maybe that is what went wrong with Peter and I. I don't know . . . but I hope I learned a lesson. Being able to turn off hurtful emotions and get on with the job is not always a good thing for a relationship. It is a bit shattering to a man's ego when you tell him that you haven't got time to cry over the row you just had because you've got three more scenes to learn.

Actress friends have always found it unusual that rather than go out on a casual date I would go home and pick up a book and spend a pleasurable evening alone. It's just that I like reading!

Chapter Eleven

My years with Charles Simon were happy ones. He is not only a very fine actor, he is a very fine laughter-maker – particularly for his fellow actors – in the most serious of scenes. "Corpsing" is the theatrical term for it; when you are made to laugh on stage when you should not. It is a somewhat childish exercise, I am ashamed to say, often employed by actors during a dull matinee or on a rainy Monday night with six in the front row.

We even managed it on *Coronation Street*, although it was not always intentional. I used to hate standing like a dummy at the bar of the Rovers and always maintained it was more natural during a long scene between other characters for me to pop off to the ladies the way people do. Only I was famous for going in the ladies and coming out through the gents. The trouble was that once off-set, there was no way of telling the two doors apart.

One of Peter Adamson's most famous lines as Len Fairclough among the cast was: "The trouble with that fellow he's got a pea like a brain."

The scene was not re-shot and the line went out and to this day I don't know why, but we did not get a single letter.

But to me Charles Simon was the master laughter-maker. He maintained it kept the younger members of the company on their toes and, in any case, it was a chance for them to learn how to deal with it.

"A good actor," he would say, "should be totally involved in his or her part and should be able to withstand anything. No matter what anyone does or says you need not laugh if you are concentrating." He would point me out to the company as a prime example of "corpse withstanding par excellence". It did not stop him trying to break me up on stage. I think I was something of a challenge.

On one momentous occasion he succeeded. It was Christmas time and we were playing *A Christmas Carol*. Charles was Scrooge, Peter was Bob Cratchett and I, for some odd reason because the part is usually played by a male, was playing the Ghost of Christmas Past, Present and Future. Charles maintained the part could be played by either sex.

I was all geared out for the Ghost of Christmas Present; so much glitter about my person I knocked everyone's eyes out. Many of the scenes were mimed and we had a small orchestra which played "God Rest You Merry, Gentlemen". Opening night the orchestra failed to turn up and all efforts to find a pianist to replace them came to naught.

Finally, a few minutes to curtain up, a very old man who was in charge of the gentleman's loo, came forward.

"Can you play 'God Rest You Merry, Gentlemen'," demanded Charles.

"Yes," quavered the old gent. "I think so."

There was no time for rehearsal and, keeping our fingers firmly crossed, we went out to face the audience. The old man sat himself down at the piano in the wings.

The scene is Bob Cratchett's departure from Scrooge's

office. I appear suddenly – as spirits are wont to do – and stand motionless at Scrooge's elbow. Charles is bent over his bowl of gruel as Peter goes into the mime. Flinging his scarf round his neck and settling his hat on his head, he gets ready to go home to his wife and family. It is the piano player's cue.

From the wings a discordant cacophony of sound assailed our ears, just discernible as a very slow and painful and truly awful rendition of "God Rest You Merry, Gentlemen". Charles lifted his head from the bowl of gruel, looked me straight in the eye and said, sotto voce and very slowly and deliberately: "He is playing the piano with his prick."

The mental picture that conjured up was too much for me. The Ghost of Christmas Past, Present and Future became a quivering, shaking mass of repressed hysterics. Peter rushed off-stage, his scarf stuffed in his mouth, and Charles, unruffled, continued to scoop gruel from his bowl.

We did the play *Random Harvest* quite often with Charles playing Smithy and me playing Paula. One night I am standing there in my Greer Garson hat and my furs, all from a local rag shop, bunch of violets in my hand, a lovely look on my face and Charles looking at me with adoration.

"Paula, do you ever regret the stage," he asks me.

"Oh, no, Smithy," my reply should have been. "They were doing our old play *Salute the Flag* at Penge last week and I passed the bills without as much as a tear."

Instead I enunciated with great clarity: "Oh, no, Smithy. They were doing our old play *Salute the Flag* at Penge last week and I pissed the bills without as much as a tear."

In a voice of equal clarity, he said: "Oh, you dirty girl," and calmly continued with his lines. Such was his insouciance, the audience did not seem to even notice.

He was full of the devil and his pet "send up" was

Random Harvest. The finale of this play is beautifully corny. Wearing a lovely dress of turquoise blue with floating skirt I would rush into his arms and say: "Oh, Smithy, Smithy, maybe it's not too late." There is a clinch as the curtain comes down.

One night I went at extra speed and bumped right into him.

"My! How your belly does tremble," he said.

Listening to the measured tones of Dr. Dale on *Mrs. Dale's Diary* I often thought how the heard but not seen media of radio must have played into Charles's delightfully wicked hands. I would listen hard, hoping to catch a glimmer of repressed laughter that meant "Charles corpsing everybody again".

A fine actor. A super, wicked gentleman – whom I couldn't fail to like.

Chapter Twelve

The years that followed went by so fast that my recollections of that period are like a trip in a time machine where one glimpses the scenery for less than a second, speeding by so swiftly you can hardly believe you have seen it. Dressing rooms, railway stations, digs, theatres, people – and half a lifetime flashed by.

So immersed in work was I that one year ran into the next without me ever noting the date. I really "didn't know what time it was". My diary held nothing but the names of plays. When I had to refer back to something it was always: "Oh, yes, that was the week we did *Rain*" or "We were in Bradford when we did *The Deep Blue Sea* (oh, yes, and I got married that week).

"It was winter when we did *White Cargo* – I remember it was cold" (who wouldn't be, wearing nothing but two strips of bright cotton and a dark tan). I was on stage practically all the time. Mind you, the lines were easy. All I had to say were things like "Tondeleyo make Tiffin" in my best cannibal island accent. Sometimes, now, I will be signing autographs in a crowd, feeling very middle-aged and respectable, and some nice old fellow, eyes alight with memories of a misbegotten youth, will whisper: "By gum! I'll never forget you as Tondeleyo."

I'll never forget me as Tondeleyo, either. Covered in tan from a bottle and shivering in every limb from the cold. We shook so much, I expect the audience thought we were all of us suffering from tropical fever.

But while I worked I dreamed. Of "making it"; the happy ending; Mr. Right. And I still listened for Heathcliff on the wind. Passing years and every week a new script. One meal a day – endless cigarettes – and half-learned scripts falling from my hands as I fell asleep with exhaustion in front of dozens of burnt-out grates.

It was at Halifax I met and made lifelong friends with Frank Redman – who was called to take so many of those on-stage photographs. Photographs to bring back so many memories.

I hardened up in those years – at least I appeared to do so. I painted a coat of aspic all over the dreamer and swapped a romantic vocabulary for hard talk and four-letter words. If I acted in the grand manner on stage, the acting I did off it was even grander – and it never stopped. I had learned the hard way that vulnerability must never show. It was a weakness – someone could put a fork through the aspic.

There was one way, though, that I never cheated. I tried always to give a fair – and what I considered to be – an honest opinion if asked for it, and frequently I was. If I thought something was wrong I would say so. I developed a reputation, which remains with me today, of being outspoken, forthright, fiery, and to hell with the consequences. If I considered something was wrong I said so, and in no uncertain terms – which doesn't mean to say I was always right.

I remember shocking a leading actor, a very pompous gentleman in love with the sound of his own voice, when I arrived late at rehearsal, full of apologies for keeping the company waiting.

"I'm sorry," I said, "I missed the bus and had to walk to work."

"My deah girl," he said, nostrils arching with distaste, "one doesn't come to work; one comes to the theatah."

"Listen, luvvy," I told him, with broad Northern accent, "I don't know what you come here to do but I come here to work."

Where direction was concerned I was not (and contrary to popular rumour, *am* not) temperamental. My temper was almost always complete fake. I used it to get results at the right moment.

Off-stage, I involved myself in all kinds of causes, lost and otherwise. I was still playing Robin Hood, I suppose. Justice for the oppressed, and all that jazz. If there was a battle to be fought I would mount my mental white charger and rush in – very often where angels feared to tread. This did nothing to enhance my reputation. Words like "firecracker", "explosive", "the Queen Bee" and "Bitch", began to follow me around. It hurt a little but it never did me any real harm.

Directors and producers who knew me well were aware that I would drive myself to the point of exhaustion endeavouring to get the characterisation they wanted. I didn't always succeed. My Mrs. Danvers in *Rebecca* was the ham performance of all time – though to be fair I had begged producer Charles Simon not to cast me in the part. But he did and the result was disastrous. Not only could I not play the part, after slapping sixteen sticks of paint all over my face in an effort to look sinister, I ended up looking like a twenty-year-old Mae West.

Those who had never met me were usually the ones to give me the titles of "bitch" and so forth. Once there was an occasion in *Coronation Street* when the regular crowd were talking of the names that used to be around in the good old rep days. We were joined by an actress who was guesting with the company for a week. I had never met her before. Charles Simon's name was mentioned.

"Oh, yes," I said. "Didn't that grotty old actress, Pat Pilkington, work for him." This for the amusement of the crowd.

"I worked with Pat Pilkington," said the actress.

"Did you?" I said, astounded.

I could not resist my next question.

"What was she like?" I dared to ask.

"A right cow," came the reply.

Well, darling, you know now, wherever you are, that Pat Pilkington and Pat Phoenix are one and the same. Lesson: Never claim acquaintance with someone you don't know. They might be listening.

My passion for principles and causes began to override my commonsense. This led me into all sorts of "beau gestes". There was one occasion when I walked out on a company, though desperately needing the money. Me and my principles and my great big mouth. We had a successful, tightly-knit company and the management were making good money (we were on about £8 a week) when they sold out to another firm. The new firm began to sort what they considered to be the wheat from the chaff. They began sackings right and left and although they offered for me and a couple of the others, they ignored many of those who had, in my opinion, made the company so successful.

They knew their own business best, but hot-head that I was, I didn't think so – and said as much. I spurned their offer. Being me I could not quietly say "no, thank you" but had to take centre stage to announce my opinions of the black-hearted villains who were taking over the theatre. It was an impassioned speech to say the least. But all it earned me was a lecture from the manager of the theatre.

"Principles are all very well, my girl," he told me, "but you're flat broke, you don't know where your next meal is coming from and you can't afford to leave."

There was only one answer to that. "I can't afford *not* to," I declared.

The burning brand fell on dry wood as I walked away. Out of the corner of my eye I saw the flicker of huge orange flames as yet another bridge caught fire and burnt behind me.

Chapter Thirteen

Looking back I don't know whether I should laugh or cry at *A Girl Called Sadie*. It was the first of the sex crime plays and when I was offered the part of Sadie, I was in two minds about whether to accept it or not.

Jack Gillam, famous outspoken Northern impressario, was taking his first venture into the straight drama and decided after seeing me as Sadie Thompson in Somerset Maugham's *Rain* that I was the only girl in the world to play (the other) Sadie. After fifteen minutes scrutiny and a fast decision I was to play the part. He then decided that Pilkington was a very unglamorous name.

"Nay, Christ, bloody 'ell (his favourite expletives with which he began every sentence) you can't go touring round the provinces with a name like Pilkington. They'll think you're selling sausages or summat. Now, what can we call ya?"

He went through several names. "How about Patricia er . . . Fleurette, or Patricia . . . er Dawn. No, wait a minute. What's that young fellow what was killed in that car accident. I know . . . Dean. James Dean. That's what we'll call you. Patricia Dean."

So Patricia Dean I became. But just for the tour.

"Sadie" was all pretty innocent stuff on today's standards but back in the fifties it caused quite a furore. Newspapers headlined "How did this play get past the Lord Chamberlain", and carried big pictures of me, hair dyed blonde, as the sultry Sadie. Once again I had been discovered. In its way it was a good part and I quite enjoyed playing it for a while, but it was such a huge success at the box office that I became imprisoned in it for months and months and began to long for release.

The run outlived the props and scenery which began to look tattier than even the squalor of Sadie's life demanded. I begged and begged for renewals, but nothing happened. One night I went on stage and tripped over a huge hole in a rug. Talk of venting your spleen on inanimate objects. Picking up the offending rug, I hurled it into the wings and screamed, still in character: "And it's time that bloody thing went in the dustbin, an' all. It's like the rest of this house. Falling apart!"

The audience saw nothing wrong but the stage manager was livid. The rug had almost hit him in the eye. My ad-libbed Sadie-style words were intended as much for the management as for the audience. I came off stage blazing.

"If I ever see that thing again I'll set fire to it," I stormed.

"Oh, dear, dear, dear," said Louis, our character man. "You're such a firebrand. Why can't you learn to be grateful."

"Grateful for what!" I spat out. "I'm giving the best work I know for a mere pittance. Why should I be grateful. This firm are not running a charitable institution. They don't give anything away."

"No," said Louis, gently. "Not that, but just grateful you are working."

I didn't understand then what he meant. I was to find out later on.

Tony Booth, who is so good as the irascible Alf Garnett's son-in-law in television's *Till Death Us Do Part*, was in the play with me. We used to send up the sex scenes sky high. I had this fabulous strip scene – very daring for those days – in which I stood before an open fireplace and dropped my dress slowly and sensuously to reveal brief black lace cami-knickers festooned with blue bows. Highly erotic! From nowhere I produced a revolver and, legs straddled like a Western gunslinger, I delivered, in my best cockney, the line: "Orl right. You've 'ad yer chance."

One night Tony crouched down behind the fireplace backstage, out of sight of the audience, and just as I delivered the line he squirted a plastic lemon right up my lace behind. I played the rest of the scene dripping with ersatz lemon juice. After that I stood as far away from the fireplace as I could. One never knew what Santa was going to spray down (or up) the chimney.

Once the run was finally over I decided to try my luck again in the big city.

I had made an earlier abortive visit to London but, thanks to Glen Melvyn, our producer at Bramhall, I did not get the chance to stay long. It was my first visit. Things were going badly with Peter and me. He had gone to London to work and I stayed home with mother in Manchester. I was determined to try my luck in London. I had about five pounds.

"You're not going down there," said mother.

"I am," I said. And I went. To London, to take the world by storm.

I booked myself into the YWCA (the only place I knew by name) and tried to think who I knew in London that I could call up. Glen Melvyn, who was by then doing very well, came to mind at once. He lived outside London at Sunbury-on-Thames.

Glen answered the phone himself.

"Hello, love," he said. "Where are you?"

"In London," I said brightly.

"What!" he exclaimed. "Are you on your own?"

I told him I was and that I was at the YWCA.

"Stay right where you are," he commanded. "I'm coming for you at once."

With admonishments not to move a muscle until he arrived, he hung up. In less than an hour he drove up in front of the YWCA.

"I'm taking you right back to Manchester," he declared. "Does your mother know you're here?"

"Glen," I protested. "I'm twenty-nine! I'm quite old enough to be in London on my own."

"I don't care how old you *think* you are, it's how old I know you are," he said firmly. And, shepherding me into the car without more ado, he took me straight back to his home where his wife, Joan, put me up for the night. The next morning he took me back to Manchester. During the drive up he lectured me on the sort of trouble I could get into in London.

"You would land in trouble in the hour," he said. "You'd be going around saying, 'Hello, isn't it a nice day' to all sorts of strange men and you can't do that here."

He handed me over to my mother with instructions not to let me out of her sight until he found me a job in London. True to his word he did. But on the very day I received his letter offering me a part in *Women of Twilight*, I had signed a six-month contract with a repertory company.

I have tremendous respect for Glen and a great deal of affection. He always treated me like a wayward child from the moment we met. I remember at Bramhall he was complaining about one of the cast ladies who was attempting to vamp everything in trousers. Glen found her obvious attempts at seduction tiresome.

"Oh, yes, I know she's supposed to be very sexy and all that but she frightens me to death," he said.

"What about me!" I hollered. "Why don't I frighten you to death. I'm supposed to be sexy, too, you know."

"Oh, you. Go away and read your story book."

I was, I suppose, a very immature twenty-nine-year-old, in spite of believing myself so sophisticated. I even remember one of the carpenters at Bramhall chastising me for using blunt language.

"Don't you ever let me catch you using language like that again," he scolded. "Them others – all right. But not you." I felt a bit deflated but at heart I was touched.

"Sadie" had caused quite a stir and this time I was sure London would fall at my feet. First we took a flat in Mornington Crescent. This proved too small for our small band of unemployed actors and actresses – all refugees from "Sadie". There was Marilyn Thomas, Bill Ridout and a couple of others. Dingy was definitely the word for it. When they were looking for a suitably squalid location for the film *Look Back In Anger* they chose to film outside our flat. It had a lovely view of the railway sidings.

Friends would drop in for a cuppa or a meal. Everyone from the rep days seemed to be out of work now or struggling. I remember Harry Littlewood and his friend Ron Taylor calling in one day. They were famished. That day we made a pound of liver and five pounds of spuds stretch between six of us.

I began the soul-destroying round of agents and auditions. All my flatmates were out of work and all of us were broke. Marilyn and I had one pair of stockings between us and whoever had the audition had got to wear the stockings. There were more auditions than parts going and, to make ends meet, we did extra work on films and in television. It seemed that all our experience and theatre technique was wasted in this job. I was resentful of TV then. It had closed so many theatres and, as an extra in crowd scenes, I would meet so many old actors and actresses that I had known and respected in the theatre; all out of work like me.

One television director, who shall be nameless, looked round the crowd and said: "Now, you lot. This is a coffee bar scene. I want you to lay about like you do in your coffee bars when you're not working."

Job or no job this was more than my fiery spirit could bear.

"You will forgive me," I said frostily. "But we are not 'you lot'. We are ladies and gentlemen, most of us very experienced in the theatre, and to my knowledge none of us have ever 'lain about in coffee bars' in our lives. But we are artists, and as such, we will give you a good performance."

Everything on the studio floor came to a full stop. There was silence. My mate, Marilyn, was pulling at my arm and saying: "Oh, crumbs, you've done it now. You'll get sacked."

There was a whispered consultation. If I had burnt another bridge – so what. It was a small span – but I still needed the job. The director walked back on to the floor.

"I'm sorry, ladies and gentlemen. I hope you will forgive me for what I said and be kind enough to act this scene for me," he said.

Was he being sarcastic? I don't know. But I do know that the next shot was a waxwork scene and close-ups were needed. Pointing to me he said: "Put the camera on that girl."

That was probably the first close-up of me on television.

Extra work on film sets sometimes turned out to be very funny and you always met up with old mates trying to make ends meet. I remember Otto Preminger's *St. Joan* at Shepperton in bitter cold weather. There were literally thousands of extras. Actors and actresses who are famous names today were togged up as French peasants. I remember Marilyn and I had two particularly hideous garments to wear. Some sort of pale blue pixie hoods with collars. There was snow on the ground and we had to dress in tents. We were herded out into the open where we waited for what seemed like hours. An Assistant Director came along with a megaphone.

"Now you lot," he shouted. "If you have any aspirations to be actors and actresses, this is how it starts. Whereupon he launched into what seemed an endless spiel about what it takes to be in the business and how to get there. I could contain myself no longer. Shrugging off Marilyn's restraining arm, I stepped forward.

"One moment please. I understand there to be another place where actors and actresses learn their craft. It is called repertory theatre. It teaches artists their business. Their *real* business, I mean, not playing about like this. And if you took the trouble to ask, you would find that is where many of the people in this crowd have been for the last few years."

"What's your name?" he demanded.

I told him. He wrote it down carefully. Marilyn was saying: "Oh, heck, you've done it again. You'll be out now."

We were rounded up on the set and Preminger said to the assistant: "Find me an interesting face or two for the close-up."

The only name he had on his board was Patricia Pilkington.

"Miss Pilkington and her friend come out here, please," he called.

And so Marilyn and I found ourselves under the scrutiny of the great Otto Preminger.

Our pixie hooded faces in close-up filled the screen for some seconds as St. Joan is burned at the stake. What cannot be seen is my torn dress. Marilyn trod on it, the skirt ripped away at the back and I was left shouting "burn the witch" in, once again, nothing but my cami-knickers. Fortunately the shot was waist level.

Not long after I was asked to play "Salome" in St. Mark's Church in Bond Street. It entails weeks of rehearsal; no money but lots of prestige – or so I was told. The performance takes place in the church itself and always draws a big crowd. I walked in for the first rehearsal to find the Stage Manager was none other than the Assistant Director on *St. Joan*. I looked at him and said: "Now, it's your turn to learn what the *theatre* is all about."

"Yes, Pat," he said.

"Miss Pilkington, if you don't mind," I told him.

I discovered his name was Joe Marks and we became great mates after that. It was a fateful meeting. He and Marilyn fell in love, got married and lived happily ever after. I like to think that they owe their happiness to me and my big mouth.

I was not always treated badly as an extra. Lionel Blair was more than kind to me, though I doubt very much he will remember. It was a musical show on television and I had been told I would not have to dance, simply stand around. But when I got there I found we were expected to do a sort of soft-shoe shuffle. Everyone mastered it with ease – except me and my two left feet. It was me, Mr. Blair, who kept saying, "I can't, I can't." I'll never forget how kind he was.

"Just come with me for a moment," he said. And, taking me to one side, he spent fifteen minutes going through the simple steps with me until I could do it. In less time than it took to teach me he could have sent me home and telephoned the agency for a more nimble-footed extra — and I would have lost a day's pay. But he didn't and I was thankful. A nice man.

Eventually I managed to get a few two-line parts on television and then a series called *You Are There* which I was in every week. It was a costume series based on historical events. The very glamorous Patricia Haynes was in it. She was always the Duchess and I was always the flower girl or the tart on the corner, with a couple of lines to say each week.

The series ended and with it, so it seemed, any demand for my services. I couldn't even get work as an extra. Coming back from the agency one day I saw a tart standing shivering on the corner. She looked as miserable as I felt. On impulse as usual I opened my purse, took out my last precious pound note and shoved it into her hand.

"Wwwhat's that for?" she stuttered in amazement.

"Oh, go and get yourself a cup of tea with it," I said. "It's a lousy life."

Chapter Fourteen

The place where I lived – or co-existed – was a seedy semi-basement flat by the railway sidings in Finsbury Park, London. My marriage had broken up and my stage career had collapsed. The bottom half of the low window blinked through its grime at dented rusting dustbins and the upper panes stared like the top half of big bi-focal spectacles at a claustrophobic curtain of mucky white cloud. There was nothing – absolutely nothing. I lit a cigarette and concluded between one smoke cloud and the next that as I did not seem to be of much use to myself – or anyone else at that particular moment – it was time for me to shuffle off this mortal coil. The decision seemed neither dramatic nor tragic to me. Just a logical conclusion that I could only become a burden and I felt I had taken enough from my mother without subjecting her to any further weight carrying. Never in my life have I felt quite the same. I have known despair and loneliness and humiliation, but I have always managed to take a gulp of fresh air and come up – if not smiling – at least fighting. On this occasion I had run out of fresh air. It was a cold, and I thought logical, decision. My main concern was that I should not leave any sort of mess or chaos behind me. So it had to look like an accident, and that would be easy.

My flatmates knew that the gas ring was sometimes blown out by the draughts and I would avoid that tell-tale ritual of packing round the door and windows with paper.

I sauntered into the kitchen, half-filled the kettle and put two spoonfuls of tea in the pot. Then I lit a match, blew it out and turned on the gas. I stroked the cat and put him outside then sat down at the kitchen table with an open copy of Thomas Wolfe's *Look Homeward Angel*. Something of a prophesy?

I fell asleep. Forty-five minutes later I coughed and spluttered myself awake to a splitting headache. The room reeked of gas but the jet was no longer hissing – it was metered and I had used what had been left of the shilling's worth. There was, I knew, no more than threepence left in my purse or, for that matter, in the world.

I started to giggle – and the giggle grew into a belly laugh. I couldn't even blot myself out properly! I mean, how could anyone be so broke that they couldn't raise a bob to commit suicide.

Later my friend, Marilyn, returned from another unsuccessful interview and, opening her big, blue eyes wide, said: "There's a bloody terrible smell of gas in here."

"Yes," I told her. "It blew out while I was making a cup of tea."

"Crikey! It could have killed you," she said.

Then, with an old fashioned look: "Hey – what are you laughing at?"

It is time to say that since, in moments of extreme stress, I have thought fleetingly, "I wish I could end it all", but only fleetingly and *never, ever* seriously after that particular incident. For I know now that spring does come round each year and tomorrow *will* be different. And how! That's half the fun of it all, isn't it?

Chapter Fifteen

But Pat Pilkington did, after all, die in London. A change of agent was what was needed I decided, and maybe it would change my luck, too. I sent off my photographs and career details to a new agent recommended by a friend. A few days later the agent's office rang.

"We're awfully sorry," said a slightly embarrassed secretary, "but the printing on the back of your photographs is a bit blurred. We can't read your last name. Is it P... something?"

Beside me on the telephone table was a book I had been reading, Marguerite Steen's *Phoenix Rising*. I took a deep breath and said: "It's Phoenix – Patricia Phoenix."

"How do you spell it?"

The voice came distantly over the wires drowned by my mind's soaring certainty, almost sounding like a rush of flame, that for the first time I had a name.

Mechanically, hardly hearing my own voice, I spelled it out, reading from the book's cover.

"P...H...O...E...N...I...X."

I hung up gently. "Phoenix, Phoenix, Phoenix," I repeated the name to myself, pleased how my top teeth touched my lower lip with the phonetics of the first syllable. A good name for a long-toothed Sagitarian, I decided. Then, as now, I believed in prophetics. It is the only name I ever felt belonged to me; not a name given me by someone else's charity, but my own. Even when I married Alan and became Mrs. Browning, I told him I would go on calling myself Pat Phoenix.

Once I went into a jeweller's shop in Blackpool in search of a gold phoenix for my charm bracelet. "May I look at your charms," I asked a rather charmless and adenoidal shop girl. "I'm looking for a phoenix."

"A what?" she queried.

"A phoenix," I repeated.

"We 'aven't got one of them," she declared. "What is it anyway?"

"A phoenix," I intoned "is the fabled bird of prophesy that immolates itself on a funeral pyre to rise again from the ashes . . ."

A vacant expression glazed her eyes and I stopped in mid-sentence.

"Oh, hell," I said. "Never mind the mythical connotations. It's a bird with a burnt bum!"

A lot of people have trouble with the spelling but it enabled me to tell my friends: "Take good care of me. There is only one of me every five hundred years."

My mother's comment when I told her of my change of name was endearingly dotty.

Said she: "Now what did you have to go and name yourself after a Dublin park for?"

I had several agents during my London days, but one I particularly remember. He was an ebullient cockney with a whippet-sharp wit whose clients, he declared, would all be stars if only they would listen to him. I was his despair.

"I want you to go to this party," he would say. "There's

a lot of important people going; blokes what'd like to meet a nice girl like you. It'll do you a lot of good in the business."

"No," was my stock reply.

"Just go and be nice to a few of the right people," he would plead. "What 'arm can it do?"

"It's prostitution and I won't do it," I would say.

He was always lecturing me on how to make it as a star and bemoaning my lack of co-operation.

"I've got anovver one just like you," he used to complain. "He won't meet none of the right people either. Never make it, 'e won't. Sings like Sinatra. 'E's good but 'e won't listen. 'E'll never listen. And 'e's got a daft name. Sounds like a poet. I've told him to change it an' all. You'll never make it, neither of you."

Today the singer with the daft name and me have a private joke. Whenever I am in the audience watching his act, Matt Monro cups his hand round his mouth and shouts: "We'll never make it!"

Sometimes it seemed as though I never would. The near-misses can be harder to take than the out and out failures. I was tested for the part of Alice Aisgill in the film of John Braine's runaway best-seller *Room at the Top*. After six or seven interviews, when I was beginning to think the part was mine, the film's backers decided they needed a "name".

It was sheer shattering heartbreak, and most actors know the feeling well, not because the part, opposite Laurence Harvey, would have undoubtedly made me a star but because I knew I *was* Alice Aisgill. I was dead right for it and I knew it. John Braine was kind enough to tell me, many years later, that if ever there was an Alice, I was it. The part went to French star Simone Signoret, and although she gave a marvellously moving performance, I still think the part called for a North Country woman.

Clochemerle was for me another miss that was as good as a mile. My agent told me they were casting a lavish London production of the famous French novel and he had suggested me for the role of the voluptuous, red-haired Judith.

I arrived at the theatre where the auditions were being held and my heart sank when I saw the queue. I got in line and pretty soon it was my turn. Wearing a sultry black dress (and if I say it myself I thought I was rather lush in those days) I walked out on to the centre of the stage and, what every actress dreams of, happened to me. From the darkened stalls the director yelled: "Hold everything!"

Magic words. My big moment!

"Christ Almighty," he ejaculated. "I've been waiting all morning for you to walk in. You are just what I want for Judith."

"This is it," I thought. "I've cracked it. I've done it. I'm in!"

His next words stopped me cold.

They were: "Where's your music?"

Stunned, I looked at him. "Music?" I said bleakly.

"Yes, yes, it's a musical," he cried.

Hopelessness flooded me. My singing voice can be likened to Tarzan's cry.

"Can't you sing at all?" wept the distraught director.

"No. No. Not a note." And I wept with him.

Selfishly I say it, there was something like a happy ending, at least for me. They never did get the show into the West End, and I never knew why. I was spared the sight of a singing Judith that might have been me. Masochistically, I would have had to have gone to the show. But for one short moment, I walked out onto that stage and knew what it felt like to be a show stopper.

If anybody had told me in those days that I would one day make not one record, but two, I would never have believed them. But I did. Both with Peter Adamson, whose vocal talents often surprise people. My first record was a kind of musical ode to *Coronation Street* which I wrote myself. Singing a song about the *Street* just would not work, so I spoke the words in Elsie Tanner's flat North Country voice with the *Street's* wistful theme song as background. It goes something like this.

Rain and more rain.
Wet roof tops,
Houses huddled together
Under a yellow blanket of smoke,
Chimneys and more chimneys,
Lights blinking on rain spattered windows,
Onto dustbins, backyards and factories.
Fading chalk on pavements,
Rope swing hanging limp from the lamp-post.
The shop, boiled ham, Beecham's Pills,
Hairnets – the pub – a pint of bitter,
Potato crisps and "mine's a small port please".
The faces, old and knowing,
Warm and young.
Expectant, disappointed, tender and tired,
The voices, soft with Northern vowels,
Where "luv" means everyone
and butties are our daily bread.
Football pools, the Halle Orchestra
and London is a foreign shore.
Sunday, and it's hot,
closing time at two o'clock.
Cushions on the doorstep,
the smell of cooking from every house.
The ice cream cart and the
Salvation Army band.

There is a warmth over everything,
an embrace, and a welcome for
this is the street – a special street.
This is Coronation Street.

I think it worked. Well, anyway, my housekeeper, Kate, cried when she heard it. Tony Warren, the creator of *Coronation Street*, was delighted with it. He threw his arms round me and kissed me.

"It's lovely, darling," he said. "But I could bash your head in for the other side."

The other side, to be fair, was well-written with a smashing backing. It was just me and my lousy voice. It was a very pubby pub song which Peter Adamson and I sang together. I didn't have the nerve to record it on my own so Peter came along to hold my hand.

We got about fourpence halfpenny in royalties for our efforts. We may have sold more if the BBC had agreed to play it, but they baulked at Beecham's Pills, claiming it was advertising and in those days, of course, there was no commercial radio. Much, much later Peter and I did a sort of Elsie Tanner and Len Fairclough to music called *The Two Of Us*. Peter did the singing which *he* is good at and I did the recitative, saying the words to music, which *I* am not so bad at.

My only other venture into song was not my idea at all. I was in rep and Christmas time and the inevitable pantomime came round. *Jack and the Beanstalk* was the manager's choice and, insisting I had just the legs for principal boy, he pushed me into playing Jack. I might have had the legs but I didn't have the voice. Come opening night and the moment for my big number and I was dreading every minute of it. I was supposed to sing "Smile" – the manager's favourite song – and he had gone out front especially to listen. I was standing in the wings with Daisy, the Cow, waiting for my entrance when inspiration struck. Always cover up with comedy, floated through my head.

"Come on," I hissed into the cow's ear. "You're coming on with me."

"What for?" came from deep in the cow's chest.

"Never mind 'what for'. Come on."

He came. It was really a case of the back half not knowing what the front half was doing. The back legs of Daisy followed trustingly onto the stage. Throwing my arms affectionately round the horns I commenced to intone (I won't say sing) in cod fashion the beautiful words of "Smile".

The boss was apoplectic. "Who told you to take that bloody cow on stage," he spluttered. I'd ruined his favourite song, he said. What did I think I was doing, he said. And much more, all punctuated by colourful Shakespearean and four-letter epithets.

I always wonder whether it wasn't him that fixed that rope ladder. Finishing the song to somewhat spasmodic applause, I bowed deeply, flung out my arm at the backcloth, slapped my thigh in the approved manner and chortled: "Goodbye, mother. I'm off to seek my fortune," and headed up the beanstalk ladder.

Halfway up it broke and I fell flat on my face. This time to tumultuous applause.

Chapter Sixteen

I go through life banging doors shut behind me only to find other doors opening in front of me. When Joan Littlewood cast me as the lead in *Fings Ain't What They Used To Be* it was a great opportunity. Not only to work at the famed Stratford Theatre, but there was a very good chance the play would go into the West End. And so it did, where it enjoyed a long run, but not with me.

I am a conventional actress trained in conventional ways and the clever routine of theatre workshop was not my cup of tea. It works for many, like Richard Harris and James Booth who were in *Fings* with me along with Yootha Joyce, but it does not agree with all artists and it did not agree with me. Miss Littlewood has done great things with many actors but I found it difficult to work in her extremely novel way of production. Mea Culpa. On the night of the dress rehearsal I was taken ill with a chest complaint and could not go on. It was some weeks before I recovered and of course I had to be replaced. Miriam Karlin took the show into the West End and both she and the show were a huge success.

One lunchtime shortly after the telephone rang. It was my agent.

"Have you played Eloise in *Tons of Money?*" he asked.

"About five years ago in rep," I replied. "Why?"

"Well, you're playing it tonight in Dublin," came the answer. "The leading lady has taken ill."

Before I had time to catch my breath, let alone worry, I was on the stage at the Olympia Theatre playing opposite Frankie Howerd. I had never set eyes on the set before my first entrance and I had hurriedly re-learned my lines on the plane over.

At the end of the run the management invited me for a drink. Teddy Palmer, my mate from way back in Bradford, and a member of the company, came along, too.

We sat around a table with the courtly Irish manager, the local priest and several others. The priest lavished praise upon my performance as Eloise. He had been very impressed he told me.

"We would like you to come back again in any play you care to choose," he said. "What would you like to do."

Without hesitation I replied *The Rose Tattoo*. Teddy kicked me under the table. The priest coloured and said in a shocked voice: "I have to tell you *that* play is not done here."

"Why not?" I said. "It's Tennessee Williams. He's done everywhere and it is a brilliant play."

Teddy, out of the corner of his mouth, was saying: "Drop it, drop it."

But the bit was between my teeth.

"Why don't you do it in Ireland?" I insisted.

"There is a certain object dropped on stage in *The Rose Tattoo*, I believe," said the priest delicately, referring to the contraceptive packet.

"Do you see the actual object?" I demanded. He had to admit you did not. I then tore into the biggest tirade ever on the dangers of keeping people in ignorance and how wrong that sort of censorship was. That I offended his sensibilities there is no doubt. I plead ignorance. He excused himself shortly and went off shaking his head. Teddy wailed: "Why didn't you choose something else? He offered you the chance of a lifetime. He'll never have you back now."

Teddy was right. I never went back to Dublin. Even as I argued I knew my words were setting light to another bridge. But I had to say what I did. I believed it to be the truth and could not pretend otherwise. Expediency has never held any appeal for me.

Back in England I was offered a part in *Happy Days* at Blackpool starring Thora Hird. At the end of the run Thora gave me a bottle of champagne.

"Aren't you going to drink it?" she asked.

"No." I told her. "I'll drink it when I make it."

That bottle of champagne remains covered in dust, tucked away on top of my wardrobe. I'm waiting for the day when I make it. The whole world may say "You are a success" but you have got to make it for yourself. I must be the judge of my own achievements. One night I may come off stage or walk off a television set one afternoon and go home and drink that champagne (if it hasn't gone sour by now). It may never happen but I know one thing. I will never stop working for it.

Chapter Seventeen

You don't give show business up, it gives you up. I had not taken London by storm and, with television closing repertory theatres up and down the country, I came home to Manchester and mother. It was 1960 and the English Rose reigned over the small screen; all beautifully cultured, well-mannered ladies they were too. It seemed there was no place for me in television. I was too big, and too ugly. I was broke and fed-up. All I had to show for my years in the business was a broken marriage and no bank balance. Being on the fringe of a business in which I had once been so involved was getting me down.

I turned to writing and spent my days tucked away, trying my hand at short stories and scripts. I shall never forget the kindness of Frank Roscoe and his wife, Joan, during those, for me, depressing times. He wrote in parts for me in a radio show called *Blackpool Nights* when I was playing in Blackpool with Thora Hird, and he encouraged me to write my own scripts as well as allowing me to ghost bits and pieces for him when he was snowed under with work. I began to do some of the *Lennie the Lion* scripts for Terry Hall and found them great fun, but not all that easy.

One had to constantly be aware of not giving Lennie or Terry manual things to do at the same time. Remembering they had only one pair of hands between them. I debated whether or not I should go back to London and it was Frank who said to me: "Don't go back to London. Go home and keep writing. I know something will turn up."

Both he and his wife, Joan, gave me a tremendous amount of help and encouragement during a period of my life when I most needed it. In my careless way I may only see them once every three years or telephone them once in every five, but I am still very much aware of the help they gave me and I shall always be grateful.

Here is one of the stories I wrote. I was tempted to tidy it up, re-write bits, tone down the odd purple passage, but I resisted. That would be cheating, so here it is, an unexpurgated original Pat Phoenix. I called it:

THE JOURNEY

The view from the train window was damp, dreary and depressing. I pressed my hot cheek against the already-misted coolness of the glass. Another train, another view – in fact, a succession of views, all looking exactly the same to my jaundiced eye. The woman with her back to the engine admonished her child, a tiny, wicked-eyed boy who was busily engaged in licking the grime from the opposite window.

"Kenneth, sit down and enjoy the nice train ride."

Train ride! I'd been on a nice train ride for the last ten years, and it had seemed like ten centuries – up and down, across the length and breadth of England, but the train was always dirty and the view always the same.

"Dirty trains, dirty towns, dirty digs," the train wheels sang to me and my weary brain took up the accompaniment. "Breathe, copulate and die – the gutter or the grave – it always has the same finale."

"Aw, Kenneth, do sit down." The woman looked across at me with a conspiratorial air. "He's a good lad, really, but when it gets past his bedtime he gets a bit fidgety."

The woman and the boy were my sole companions on the long journey South.

"He's only four, y'know – usually in bed by seven."

This, I thought, is where I get the child's history from the womb up to his last cute saying.

"He's a funny kid, though. 'Course, you can't wonder – I had such a bad time when he was born."

She was away and I was trapped for at least an hour. I settled my features into an interested and what I hoped was an intelligent expression.

"Really," I said.

"Aw yes,'" she replied. "I was forty-eight hours in labour."

Labour – Labour – Labour, sang the train.

"Labour," I thought. "Pain, lust, sex – sex." I stopped.

Sex? Someone had wanted, desired, the woman opposite me. An ugly giggle rose in my throat. I swallowed it back. She was gross; her bolster-shaped breasts sagged away to the outer perimeter of her swollen, soft body; her ankles oozed over the tops of her sensible shoes. My eyes fled to her face – the eyes ice chips and blubber; the nose, just flesh; the mouth small and tight; the hair black, unwashed, almost wig-like.

"Then at two he 'ad the 'ooping cough."

The child, sensing himself the centre of attention, had stopped trying to strangle himself with the window strap and turned his pointed, fawn-like face towards me. It was hard to believe that this small satyr issued in love, lust or erotic desire from the loins of the creature who was now regaling my defenceless ears with his life history.

"But some of the things you read in the Sunday papers make you squirm, really they do."

Another topic! Suddenly I wanted to see her squirm.

Suppose I said suddenly, "I have just been to bed with a man – and guess what? He was married . . . but not to me. That's better than the Sunday papers, isn't it?"

She would laugh and think I was joking. But I would not say it and she would continue to chatter to me for no better reason than the delusion that I was respectable. Respectability! – the cloak of the God-fearing, man-fearing, run-with-the-pack masses.

"And when the police got there they found the 'ouse in a filthy state."

Like Tennyson's brook, she babbled on. The boy's narrow, heavy-lashed eyes found mine.

"Like his," I thought, "like the eyes of my lover –"

"Lover – Lover – Lover."

My nipples ached, remembering. The boy smiled at me.

Tenderness came – a sun-warmed shower. Maternity. All men are as little children.

I jerked back my wandering thoughts. The woman chattered on. Somehow she had changed. No longer fat and ugly – just big and pleasant, a mother, and this the child of her womb – the fruit of a respectable marriage. She has so much more than I!

"She's pretty," said the boy, staring at me. "She's all soft and her hair's pretty." He reached up to touch my hair. The woman pulled him back.

"Kenneth, don't be rude," she said.

"I'm not," he said. "It's like – it's like – it's like a bonfire."

He had said that – my lover. No! My ex-lover.

"Hair like fire, a body made for love." But he had meant lust and it had taken me three months to discover what he meant, four months to discover that he loved his wife and lusted after me. So this afternoon had seen the last of hotel bedrooms for a while.

Dirty towels, dirty trains, dirty digs – the train giggled.

Who was it said that the spirit is willing, the flesh is weak?

What the mind rejected, the heart and flesh still desired.

I had said, "This is the last time." I was so strong, but why did my body keep remembering his hands; why could I still taste his sweat on my tongue?

"Lover – Lover – Lover – Mistress."

"You see, my darling, I've been married for ten years and I wouldn't want to hurt her ... You're the most wonderful ... My son is six years old ... Your breasts are so soft – kiss me ... It's his birthday on Saturday, so I can't be with you this week-end. Kiss me! You are the most wonderful ... It's so hot ... Darling, darling, darling."

Oh God! Mistress mine where are you roaming?

"Oh darling." Then the train. "Don't wait 'till it goes, let's say 'Goodbye' now." His slim length retreating down the platform.

So there would be no small satyr of my own, no long-eyed goblin to enchant strangers on the train – the dirty train, the week-end express.

"You'll excuse him, ma'am, but you *are* pretty. And out of the mouths of babes and sucklings, they say."

The woman had lifted the boy on to her knee. Now she became beautiful; a Madonna; the ring on her left hand was pure gold – (pure gold – pure gold – pure gold! Pure) Chastity! No furtive week-ends! A son just four years old, born in holy wedlock. I envied her. She was a goddess and I was — a mistress!

My eye became warmer as did her conversation. I basked in her soothing golden babble for thirty miles. There must be some men then who loved for love's own sweet sake? This woman had never been taken in angry lust for the sake of a beautiful body.

The train slowed down. A station. She set down the boy and, collecting her belongings about her, "This is where I get out," she said. "It's been loverly talking to you, as if I'd known you all my life." She opened the carriage door. "Of course, the big regret of my life is that his dad and me was never married."

The door closed behind her, the whistle blew, the train carried me on into the night. The window of the train was cool against my hot cheek.

Chapter Eighteen

I tapped away on the typewriter; the weeks stretched on, the telephone stayed silent. This was the end, I told myself. Miss Phoenix had taken her final bow. But the curtain had not fallen on the final act. In the best of traditions the hour is darkest before the dawn. And my dawn came with a call from Granada television.

They wanted an interviewer with a warm touch for what was then a small lunchtime chat show seen only in the North called *People and Places*. If I wanted it the part was almost certainly mine. It was not the biggest break in television history, but for a lady who had been turned down by countless television producers for being "too busty" and "too passionate" it was a start.

Then someone told me about this *Florizel Street* thing. It was a North Country drama to run thirteen weeks, once a week, and only in the North. No one got very excited. The buzz began that Granada were thinking of showing it twice weekly and it might be shown in other regions. Every actor born anywhere near the North rushed to audition. Over five hundred were seen and, although nobody knew it then, a handful were to be sifted out for world-wide acclaim. I reacted to this unseemly scramble for parts in my typically aggressive way.

"*Another* audition. No, thank you!"

I remember telling my mother quite firmly, "I'm not going."

My friend and one-time agent, Mrs. Mullings, Bill Nadin and my mother all exerted pressure on me.

"You must go – you must. If only to show your face."

"Who wants to see my face," I muttered darkly.

Little did I know – as they say in melodrama.

I had my chat show and that was enough for me. I did not have to *be* anything I told myself. I suppose, in reality, I had got beyond hope; almost given up.

But an appointment had been made for me and reluctantly I went, telling myself what a waste of time it all was. Bill made sure I travelled in style by taking me in his taxi, but my mood was truculent. I was like the poor farmer who lives next door to a rich farmer and wants to borrow his neighbour's plough. On the way over to ask for it he thinks: "Tom's a good bloke, he'll lend me his plough when he knows mine's broken. He's got two, anyway. Hmmm, wish I had two."

By the time he's gone half-way it begins to rain and he's getting a bit tired.

"Why should he have two ploughs, anyway," he thinks. "I haven't got two ploughs. It's probably not a very good plough. In fact, it's probably a lousy plough."

By the time he gets three-quarters of the way there he's soaking wet and thoroughly fed up.

"I bet he won't lend it to me after I've walked all this way," he thinks.

"Well, I don't care if he doesn't. Who does he think he is with his two ploughs."

By the time he gets to the rich farmer's he's in a thoroughly aggressive mood.

He works himself up into such a state that, by the time the rich farmer opens the door to him, he shouts: "And you can keep your bloody plough!"

Such was my mood when I walked in to audition for Granada; the first of the anti-heroines.

Six people faced me instead of the one I had expected. I muttered deliberately, audibly, "Oh, bloody 'ell," and flashing a furious look from under my eyebrows, flopped into a chair in front of them. They started with their questions.

"What have you done before, Miss er . . ."

"Thousands of years," I replied bitterly from my slumped position.

Eyebrows shot up and one of the six, a tall, blond, willowy youth, giggled.

"What the hell is that boy doing here," I wondered, completely unaware that I was looking at the creator of what was to turn out to be one of the most successful series ever; someone who was later to become one of my best friends, the brilliant, erratic, outrageous *enfant terrible* of television, Tony Warren.

They gave me a script folded over and asked me to read. "Yeah, all right," I drawled. We could all play the wasting time game. One of them, I can't remember which, read the other part and I began.

We were not used to television dialogue that sounded like real people in those days. Ladies on television then were "awfully naice" and had nicely rounded vowels to match. I could see if there was anything rounded about Elsie Tanner it wasn't her vowels.

After I had read for them the blond youth asked me if I would mind standing up and removing my coat. Cheeky young devil, I thought.

"No," I said flatly. "You'll just have to guess at it, won't you?"

I'd be damned if I would parade for them. I had been to too many auditions and lost too many good parts to take this lot seriously. My drawbridges were up that day but through the moat of indifference began to filter the notion that what I had just read was good. It was more than good. It was a glorious, gutsy, gift of a part and I wanted it, but I thought I didn't stand a cat in hell's chance of getting it after the aggressive performance I had given.

Unwittingly I had been in just the right mood for the scene and the character and had played it well. But I did not wait to hear their verdict. With a resigned "Don't phone me, I'll phone you" I walked out of the door. I had burned another bridge – or so I thought.

But then came a telephone call and a confirming letter. I had got the dry runs – that is to say they were trying me out for the part. I was absolutely over the moon. In spite of my "couldn't care less" attitude, I got the part. Thank God they could see through it. I did all the things that one should never do at an audition. If I had gone in with my best posh interviewing voice telling them "actually I have done this that and the other and wasn't I jolly super" I would have killed the whole thing stone dead.

There had been controversy over my age. Some said I was too young, which I was at the time, but fortunately I was carrying too much weight. They decided to age me by lining me with make-up on the cheeks and forehead. They could have waited! It didn't take me long to catch up. After a couple of weeks and little by little I left the bits off and it was accepted. People are often puzzled because I look something like the same on television now as I did thirteen years ago.

I was supposed to be ten years older than I was and the

extra weight I was carrying helped. I was asked not to diet at first but, as the years went on I managed to shed most of it. I had to be careful about too drastic dieting; once I went on a crash diet and letters poured in from male admirers, who liked a bit of something to grab hold of, begging me not to lose any more weight.

But that was a long time after the cold winter of 1960 when, for the first time, I met the rest of the group of unknown actors who were destined to become world famous and some my very good friends. I was delighted to see among the little group of strangers a dear and familiar face. We had known each other for years and often met in television studios, when both of us were doing extra work and little bits and pieces. It was Doris Speed, now almost equally well-known by the name of Annie Walker.

Although I was told I had the dry runs, nobody actually came to me and officially told me I had the part for keeps. Right up to the last minute I was on tenterhooks and finally I asked the director, Mike Scott, who was amazed.

"Of course, you've got it," he said.

For the first time I allowed myself a feeling of real elation.

Tony Warren, the young trainee writer from Salford who created the series, had taken the names of the characters – Tanner, Sharples, Tatlock, Barlow – from tombstones in a local cemetery.

When Granada read the first of his scripts they were not enthusiastic. Too dreary, they thought, and how would the rest of the country react to the Northern accents. But I had a feeling – more than that, I knew.

"If anybody sees this thing it will take off." It was different, it was truthful and it had acid in it. For the first time Northerners were shown to have passion. It was almost Italian in its earthy delivery.

During rehearsals the name was changed after the cleaning lady told Tony Warren that *Florizel Street* sounded like a disinfectant. They argued for two whole days about a new name and finally put all the suggestions into a hat and drew one out. *Jubilee Street* had been strongly favoured but it was *Coronation Street* that came out of the hat and *Coronation Street* stuck.

Coronation Street – with its now familiar rows of smoking chimneys and haunting theme music – went out live for the first time on December 9th, 1960. Its leading actors were shaking in their shoes and its clever young author was so nervous he was being sick in the loo. Those critics who bothered to review it were quite kind, only one stuck his neck out and said it was dreary, it would not be a success. But it was – right from the start the viewers loved it and the letters that piled in at every post proclaimed it.

It was hard to believe at first when the cheering and the fan mail started. But one rainy winter's night when everyone had gone home, Peter Adamson and I were standing together at the studio's fourth-floor window looking out over the lights of Manchester.

Suddenly I turned to him and, choking for some strange reason, said: "Peter. It belongs to us."

"By God, chuck," he said, throwing an arm over my shoulder. "You're right. It does."

We stood, two people silhouetted against the brilliantly wet streets of the old city, only just guessing at what fate had in store.

Chapter Nineteen

Coronation Street quickly established itself as a firm favourite with viewers in the North. In television parlance it "took off" and there could not have been a more intoxicated load of passengers; intoxicated with delight and success. From March, 1961, it was shown in other parts of the country where it proved equally popular. In the summer it soared into the top ten of the ratings where it has remained practically ever since.

Thirteen years of playing Elsie Tanner on television twice a week has inured me to people who confuse the real me with Elsie. If that's what people want to believe, let 'em. But in the beginning I spent a lot of time writing to people and explaining that I didn't really live at Number Eleven Coronation Street. *I* still believe in the knight on the white charger so, if the world wants to believe in Elsie Tanner, God bless 'em. They pay me a compliment.

It *is* confusing when my real life husband, Alan Browning, played my TV husband, Alan Howard, and it is not surprising the edges of reality got a bit blurred. There was a moment when I had a row with my TV husband Alan about dishing up endless fish and chips and sausages and mash.

"Why can't we have something different like corn on the cob," the script had him complaining.

The very next day after the episode was screened, I opened a supermarket and women flocked around me pushing tins of corn on the cob into my hand and voicing their disapproval of my behaviour.

" 'Ere. Don't be so awkward. Give 'im corn on the cob if he wants it," they insisted.

We had corn on the cob for breakfast, lunch and dinner that week.

And when an old Lancashire lady stopped me in the street and said: "You were nowty with Alan last night. You'll lose 'im the way you carry on." It was absolutely second nature for me to say: "Yeah, I know, luv. I'm sorry but I 'ad a bit of an 'eadache."

There is a certain breed of child that appeals to me more than all others; the ones with freckles and slightly protruding teeth. I shall never forget a small kid about ten years old who had watched me as I waited outside the studios, chin tucked into mink coat, on a bitterly cold night for a car that was taking me to a personal appearance. His eyes followed me as the car (which did not belong to me) swished up and the chauffeur opened the door for me. The boy stepped forward – nose a little blue with cold, thin coat drawn around him.

"It's all wrong you know," he said.

"What's all wrong?"

"You're supposed to be poor," he said. "Living in a street like Coronation Street and look at that coat. And what about this posh car."

I had to do some quick thinking. I answered as sincerely as I could.

"Now just a minute," I said. "I've been standing in that doorway in the freezing cold waiting for this car that's going to take me somewhere important. I've got to be there in half an hour and I won't get there on the bus, will I? And if I stood in a doorway signing your rotten autographs without a coat like this I'd catch my death of cold and couldn't go on Coronation Street, could I? Eh?"

He looked at me with understanding beyond his years, tapped his finger to his head and said briskly: "Point taken, Mrs. Tanner."

We parted with mutual grins of respect.

But it is not just children and old ladies who have trouble separating our screen selves from our real selves. Philip Lowrie, who played my saucy son, Dennis, accompanied me on a personal appearance at a cinema once. I was "all got up" in a floor length gown, sequins blazing, and Dennis wore a smoothly expensive dinner suit. We could not have looked less like the Tanner family if we had tried, which come to think of it we had. Crowds were lining the entrance and as Philip and I stepped from the car, a woman ducked under a policeman's arm and fetched Philip a walloping backhander. He reeled back and she shouted: "That's for being so bloody cheeky to your mother."

She disappeared back into the crowd and poor Philip spent the whole evening with an angry weal across his face.

We have all, at some time or other, suffered in varying degrees from that sort of violence, and have come to accept that, at times, we are targets. I have never believed in losing contact with the background from which I came – a sort of basis for Coronation Street. On odd occasions we visited Yates's Wine Lodge in Manchester. One Sunday lunchtime Alan and I walked in for a quick drink. We were sitting in a corner when a friendly-looking old man came up.

"You're 'er, aren't ya? 'Er on the telly," he said.

Before I could say a word he punched me hard in the

shoulder and vanished before Alan could do a thing to intervene. In contrast I met a lovely old gentleman not long ago who, shaking with emotion, said: "I'm eighty-odd. I've come forty-six miles. I caught the seven o'clock bus to come and see you. I think you're the most marvellous woman I have ever met in my life."

He had tears in his eyes and I don't mind admitting I was choked up. I just put my arms around him and kissed him.

"You're not so bad yourself," I told him with genuine emotion.

I go among crowds completely freely. They are only people and I am one of them; I believe in them for they pay me the compliment of believing in me. It sometimes happens in a crush when people press close to you that your arms literally disappear into the crowd as people grasp your hands. The majority are lovely, loving people but you get the occasional nutcase in the frantic crush that bends your fingers back 'till you think they are going to break. Thank God, they are in the minority.

Easier to deal with are the bottom pinchers. I just step back smartly and grind my heel into their instep. If they are youths doing it for a lark, and this is usually the case, and I catch them at it, I say: "Listen! I can give our Dennis a thick ear for less than that. You're asking for trouble."

They laugh; take the point and usually apologise with the best of humour.

"Sorry, Elsie. Sorry, Mrs. Tanner," they grin.

Out of the crowds come back memories of many different faces; "old and knowing, warm and young, expectant, disappointed, tender and tired". One such face is etched more clearly than any on my memory. An old lady with her hair scraped back and an obviously threadbare coat clasped around her. I don't know why but perhaps, with her shopping bags, standing in the pouring rain, the steam coming off the crowd in Liverpool at ten o'clock on a Monday morning, she seemed so typical. My grandma, Alan's grandma, your grandma, everybody's grandma. As I stepped out of the car she opened a very soiled piece of paper and said: "I've got up at the crack of dawn and I've travelled ninety miles to get here. Now you'll bloody sign that."

I bloody did – with pleasure.

The public often find it amusing when I appear to lose my temper. "A bit of fire" they call it. In every crowd the children are always at the front and if there is any pushing or bad behaviour it is always the children who get hurt first. I see it happening and hide behind Mrs. Tanner's volcanic vocabulary.

"Any more of that flamin' shoving and I'll come among you and sort you all out – and don't think I'm not capable."

This is invariably met with a gust of good-natured laughter.

"That's our Elsie. Eee, she's at it, again."

In the early days Peter Adamson, as Len Fairclough, had some lines to say really knocking Elsie.

He read through them and said to me: "I'm not saying that speech. I'll get lynched."

His nervousness was not surprising. He had just been punched on the nose in a pub by a man who said he was fed up with Len throwing his weight around in the Rovers Return.

Peter once said that if I appeared on the screen doing a Harvey Smith, the public would nod their approval and feel they were being let in on a great "Elsie" joke. I am not so sure he was right but, to my delight, the great heart of Elsie Tanner, born in Tony Warren's scripts and nurtured every day by my own mother, found an answering place in the hearts of the public. I believe in every winner there is a loser. The public sensed in Elsie – and in me for that matter – that this was so. It applies to most women in this great big wide world and it is on this bridge we meet and identify.

Elsie is to men, or so I am told, a bit of alright, the sex symbol next door, the woman every Joe Bloggs can tell himself would be "alright on a foggy night for a quick fumble". To nice old ladies she is the daughter they never had, perhaps lost. One old lady who has been writing to me for years always addresses me as "My Queen".

"Now, My Queen", she writes. "Last night you were a bit hasty. You must learn to control that temper of yours. It is always getting you into trouble."

I get the feeling that I am a sort of daughter in a way; that I am substituting. And I am very glad to do so.

It is not by any means everybody that approves of Elsie Tanner. I once got a rather disagreeable, if not snotty, letter from six typists who all worked in the same office. Six typists they were and six typists they signed themselves. They objected to a scene where, draped only in a nightie, I leaned out of the window to call to Dennis in the street below. By sheer accident the camera was at an angle and the shot was almost down to my naval. Some people would say "a lot of charisma", others would say "a big boob shot". The six typists were indignant. "Outrageous" and "Obscene" they called it. There was really only one answer. So I wrote back "Jealous" and signed it Pat Phoenix.

Chapter Twenty

We were all of us a little shaken when we began to realise that the Street and its inhabitants were thought of as real by a large part of the public. They began to write to me – or rather Elsie Tanner – not only to give advice to her, which I could cope with, but to ask advice on their personal problems, which I could not. I could not presume to advise in areas where it was patently obvious professional help was needed. All I could do was to write back and tell them to talk to their doctor, or lawyer – whoever was more fitting.

We began to receive gifts, too. Bottles of stout for Ena, and one Chinese family from Limehouse sent me money after Dennis had pinched from my purse. It was written in pidgin English and said:

"Dear Elsie, we velly much like watch *Coronation Street*. If Ena Sharples nasty we cut off her head and stick it on top of telly. Please find enclosed one pound English note to pay for money Dennis steal."

Vi thought this very funny.

I could not spoil it for them by sending the money back so I gave it to a charity instead.

The very new look. Happy days at Keighley.

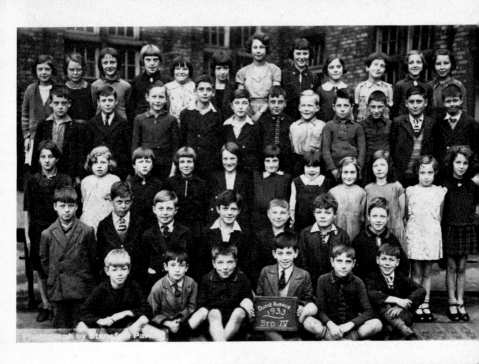

Above: Ducie Avenue
Municipal Mixed Infants.
Top right: It must have been
someone else's cardigan.

Right: *When Knights Were
Bold*. I even sang in this one.

Above: *Poor Dad* at Lancaster, playing a juvenile delinquent.

Below: With Hugh Wallington in *Shining Hour* at Lancaster.

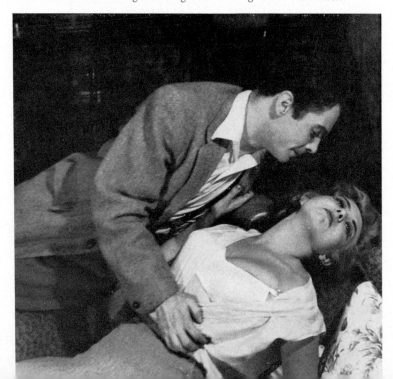

Right: Sadie Thompson in *Rain*. Just look at those sub-standard nylons.

Below: Lola in *Come Back, Little Sheba*.

Above: With ex-husband Peter in a play I forget.

Below: A mum's part. Me, Gillian and Hughie Wallington.

Playing Peter's mum in *Black Chiffon*.

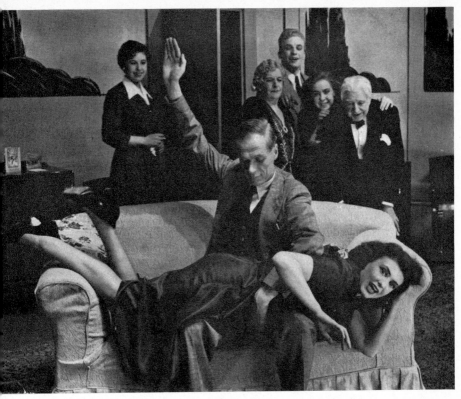

Above: *Friendly Relations*. I got my own back. I bit his leg.

Below: Don Sutcliffe and me at Halifax.

Wedding No. 1.

Tondelayo in *White Cargo*. Goose pimples and my mum's horse-brass.

Above: Doris, Arthur and me at the bar.

Left: Miss Gossage in *The Happiest Days of Your Life*.

The big day: Doris, Arthur, Mr. and Mrs. Wilson, Jim and me.

Below: Triumphant entry into Adelaide.

The David Frost Show.

Above: Bill, Alan, me, Alan's daughter Mamie and H.V.K.

Below: Can I sign it Phoenix-Browning please?

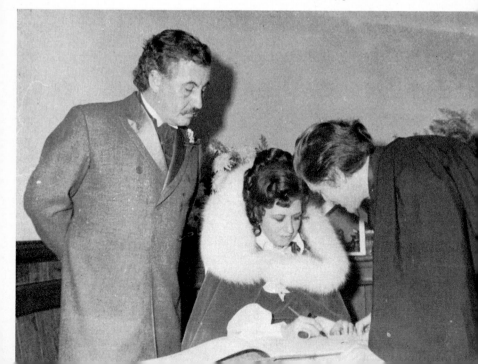

Ada's cake.

Right: The boss, relaxing.

Below: The four of them, the two of us. Blackie, Joe, Bossy and Chips.

That year the *Street* had its first wedding and it un-leashed flowers, telegrams, telephone calls and gifts galore from viewers for the couple, Harry Hewitt and Concepta, the Rovers barmaid; in real life Ivan Beavis and Doreen Keogh. That year saw the *Street's* first funeral, too – Ida Barlow – it brought a rash of wreaths for the very much alive Noël Dyson.

When she left, she bought the *Street* a farewell present; a plant in a pot which we installed in the rest room, or, as actors call it, the Green Room. It was a creeper and, true to its name, it crept and crept and crept and is still creeping. Now, thirteen years later, it is halfway across the ceiling, clinging to a trellis I bought for it, and known affectionately by the company as "Dear Quatermass". No plant in history can have had the love and attention which is lavished on it to such a degree. Fed, watered, nourished and nurtured on tender care, it thrives. We take it in turns to re-pot it and last time I bought a nice urn and one of the carpenters came up and bored some holes in it for me. During an elec-tricians' strike, when *Coronation Street* was off the air, we took it in turns to risk an industrial dispute by sneaking into the building and watering the plant. We have a special reason for concern. There is a superstition grown up among the cast that if that plant dies so will *Coronation Street*. If somebody told me it was dying, even though I have left the *Street*, I would hire half-a-dozen gardeners to attend it. Someone once asked me if I would go back to *Coronation Street* to save the plant. A cryptic question. My answer was: "Yes. I'd go back and water it."

Had the realism gone too far, we wondered, when we got wreaths for Noël, but we swiftly became inured to it. Our ever-thorough producers had fixed the controlled rents of the houses in the *Street* at a realistic nineteen shillings. When one became vacant hundreds clamoured to rent it.

We had requests to hire the back room of the Rovers for office parties and two builders sent estimates when the licensees, Jack and Annie Walker, talked of having the place done up. When the script had them thinking about moving to another pub several viewers wrote in and said they knew the Rovers well and asked how to go about applying for the licence.

I was opening a block of new council flats in Leeds and there must have been a crowd of 6,000. A little old lady sidled up to me after it was over and said: "Don't fret love. When you've waited a bit they'll have you out of *Coronation Street* and you'll have one of these for yourself."

This confusion in viewers' minds brought its responsibilities. Ena Sharples went into the shop and complained: "That potted meat was off."

We got anguished letters from small shopkeepers pleading with us not to say that sort of thing. None of them had sold any potted meat the week that episode went out.

The simplest scripted remark can enrage even today. Hilda Ogden and her Stan were commiserating with each other about their need of a holiday abroad and lack of funds to pay for it. "We can't even afford the fare to rotten New Brighton," said Hilda. The town and its supporters were up in arms at what, I am sure, the scriptwriters had intended as no slur but simply a "Hilda-ism".

We not only had to be careful of what we said, but of what we did. Elsie Tanner once brought a factory to a grinding halt for the whole morning at a cost of hundreds in lost man hours; and all because she had a night out on the town with a mate.

At an engineering works in Salford two fellows working side by side on a bench began chatting about the episode of the night before: "By, it was good last night," said one.

"Them two. Elsie and Dot on the town. Getting drunk. I allus like Elsie. I think she's smashin'."

"Elsie Tanner! That old bag. I wouldn't give 'er 'ouse room," said his mate.

That started it! Before anyone knew what was happening they were at it, fists flying. The foreman came round to find out what was going on.

" 'E called Elsie Tanner an old bag," he was told indignantly.

"He said what!" cried the foreman.

And before anyone knew it the whole factory was battling it out. When it all calmed down the Managing Director sent for the two ring-leaders. I would loved to have been there when he asked for an explanation. Can you imagine?

"Now what is this all about, chaps?" from the Managing Director.

A pause.

Employee: "Well, he called Elsie Tanner an old bag."

Managing Director: "Who may I ask is Elsie Tanner?"

Employee: "Well, it's 'er out of *Coronation Street*."

A work stoppage and all over someone who did not really exist!

Elsie caused more than one fight in her time. I'll never forget poor Jack Watson who was playing a sailor on the make for her. But he was dealing her a double line and everybody but Elsie knew he was married. One morning Jack was coming along Deansgate to the Studios when he passed a couple of dustbin men. Suddenly one of them shouted.

" 'Ere! You're 'im, aren't ya?"

Before Jack could say a word he found himself pinned against the wall and a menacing face shoved up to his.

"Now, do bloody right by 'er or I'll get ya, wack," said this beefy dustbin man.

Jack came into the studio pale and visibly shaken. He was not looking forward to going home that night either because they had threatened to wait outside for him.

I was enormously touched how this affair sparked off concern for Elsie. Shortly after Jack was threatened I made a personal appearance and as I stood signing autographs and chatting to people at the end of a long hall I saw two little lads racing towards me. They came bursting up and when they reached me panted: "Elsie, he's married. He's married. Did you know he's married?"

All I could say was that I hadn't heard and I would have to look into it when I got home.

A farm labourer from an improbable sounding place in the depths of the country like Starkader Mains, wrote and offered to take me away from it all. He said he had enough to keep me in comfort – he earned twenty pounds a fort-night – and we could live together beautifully on that.

It was very romantic. He said every night I could make him cow heel pie and we would sit and watch me on *Coronation Street* together. How I was supposed to be making him cow heel pie *and* appearing on television at the same time, he did not explain.

Not all the proposals I received were so romantic. For years I got this same letter every week from a man with the oddest pseudonym whose touch for the erotic turn of phrase was, to say the least, inventive. It became a company joke. Kenneth Cope, who was playing Jed Stone, would put his flat cap on, sidle up to me every morning at rehearsals and very sleazy like, out of the corner of his mouth, mutter: "Get my letter this morning, then?"

The boys all thought it was a great joke and used to pass it around among themselves. Finally one morning dear Violet Carson – who is as unlike Ena Sharples as it is possible to be – said: "Can I see the letter, Pat?"

"Oh, no, darling," I said. "You don't want to see it. You're much too young."

"Oh, I think I should," she insisted.

So I passed it over to her and she began to read it. First she gasped, then she went "tut, tut", then she gasped again and finally she laughed.

"Hmmm," she said. "He's boasting a bit, isn't he?"

Violet had then, and still has today, a lovely sense of humour.

My letter writer got quite romantic towards the end and finished up proposing to meet me under the clock at Waterloo Station wearing a red carnation so I would know him. The whole cast of *Coronation Street* were in favour of turning up all wearing red carnations. Needless to say I did not turn up and that was the last of my pornographic knight errant. The boys claimed they missed him, but I can't say I did.

My old mate, Bill Nadin, used to have a collection of the more bizarre letters I received. The really insulting ones we got we would pin on the studio notice board, which is the best thing to do with letters like that. Each of us gets a stack of letters every day but it seems like it is always the morning when you are feeling a bit squeamish that you get the erotic mail. Ten o'clock in the morning is not the time to do a quick study of the male anatomy – and not very pretty at that!

The one that got me screaming, but with laughter, came from a vicar. It read: "Dear Madam, My organ has recently collapsed and I would like your assistance in raising it."

A letter like that is always read out loud to the company and nobody believed me until they saw it for themselves. But it was genuine enough. He wanted me to attend a fete and help raise money for the church organ. That one became a *Coronation Street* classic.

Chapter Twenty-One

Coronation Street gave us all money to spend. For the record, let us state here and now, once and for all – I am hopeless with money. I behave with it in the manner of the Red Indians of Manhattan and treat it like beads.

"How lovely! Here, you have some and you have some. Oh, I forget, did someone say I have to pay taxes?" Daft, I tell you!

But I believe the more possessions you get the more laboured down you are with looking after them. It seems to be my goal in life to get rid of money as soon as I get it; not intentionally, but it just seems to happen. My mother was always saying I would never have a penny to my name and it is true – I never will. However hard I try to make a fist around my cash, my fingers remain forever open.

For some on the *Street* the good life came a little late. Too many years of scraping along on small salaries, too many years more out of work than in. Success they could cope with, but excess came harder. The late Arthur Leslie, who died so tragically while on holiday in 1970, made few concessions to his new-found fortune. He was ready to retire when he was cast as Jack Walker, licensee of the

Rovers, in 1960, and apart from moving into a comfortable house in Blackpool with his wife, Betty, and beloved peke, Lulu, his only other extravagance was to travel first class on the train from Blackpool to Manchester every day to work. And he did not do that until he signed his first two-year contract and began to believe the prosperity might be here to stay.

Jack Howarth was one of us who was more in work than out of it, in spite of the fact he had only played in two series in twenty-seven years. Before his casting in 1960 as Albert Tatlock in the *Street*, he played Mr. Maggs in *Mrs. Dale's Diary* on radio for fourteen years. He and his actress wife, Betty Murgatroyd, are a devoted couple who spend their working weeks in Manchester's Midland Hotel and weekends at their lovely North Wales bungalow.

People are often surprised to find that Jack has no moustache in real life. He is clean-shaven and always has been. He admits it would be easier to grow a real one and save sticking on a false one every time, but claims he "doesn't fancy himself with a moustache". But he did fancy Albert Tatlock with one; "small and bushy" he insisted and argued with the producers until he got his way. When they saw the first run-through they admitted he was right, and Albert kept his tash.

Jack and I have this little secret. For years we have been having this totally imaginary, but very passionate affair. Every Thursday afternoon at three o'clock he threatens to tell me how you get babies.

"Oh, you and your promises," I always tell him. Seriously though, he's lovely and I love him dearly. It's hard to imagine Jack without the little blue cornflower he wears in his lapel. I don't know how he manages it, but he seems to have a fresh one for every day of the year.

I don't think *Coronation Street* has changed Violet Carson

or her way of life. She still lives with her sister in a bungalow on the outskirts of Blackpool. Violet may not have changed but the house has had to. She would just be getting ready to do a little pruning on her roses when there would be a squeal of brakes and a large bus-load of tourists, from as far away as Australia, would pull up outside her front door.

"And this," the conductor would announce with a grandiose wave of the arm as if he were pointing towards Buck House, "is the 'ome of the celebrated Ena Sharples."

There would be much craning of necks out of the bus windows. Enough is enough, decided Violet, and turned her house back to front. Her kitchen faces the street and her sitting room now overlooks the back garden. And to think someone wanted to cut Ena Sharples out of *Coronation Street* altogether.

None of the actresses auditioned for the part was right and the producers despaired of finding anyone. "Let's leave Ena out," they suggested. Tony Warren, the series creator, was adamant in refusing.

He maintained, rightly, every street has a woman like Ena. In a flash of inspiration he thought of Violet Carson, who he knew from his days as a child actor on the BBC when she had played the piano and sung. Nobody was quite sure she would be interested in the role and Granada debated whether it was worth paying her fare from Blackpool for the audition.

When Violet read the script her verdict on Ena Sharples was "just an old back street bitch". Gentle, musical Violet thinks that Tony thought of her for the part because he was a dreadfully precocious child and she was always threatening to smack his bottom, which he readily admits he deserved.

Violet's hair is crisp and short and curly and very, very

pretty. And that is the reason for those two heavy hairnets which adhere so grimly to her brow. They serve to hide that attractive silvery hair. Without the hairnets and the old coat she is the perfect lady; charmingly mannered and rather regal, very much the Queen Mother. Once, when we were on the Royal Command performance, Michael Bentine desperately wanted to speak to Violet whom he had never met, but she was deep in conversation with somebody else.

"How do I get to speak to her?" he asked me.

"It's simple," I told him. "Just touch her lightly on the elbow, address her as Ma'am and when she turns round, drop her a curtsy."

And that is exactly what he did. Violet looked at him in amazement and said: "What *are* you doing down there?"

When he told her she hooted with laughter.

Darling Doris Speed, like Violet, is totally unlike the snappy snob she portrays on screen. Quite the reverse. She lives in a small semi-detached house near the studios and still comes in on the bus if she feels like it. She is a great wit and it is typical of her that when she bought her first mink coat she called it "Tony" in tribute to Tony Warren who, as the writer of *Coronation Street*, helped put the mink on all our backs.

I remember once, in the early days, making a personal appearance at a factory just after passing the milestone of my first mink.

I was wearing it, of course, and one of the factory girls stroked it dreamily and said: "Oh, Miss Phoenix, what a smashin' bit of fur."

"Go on," I told her. "Try it on."

Before anyone knew what was happening that coat had gone all down the assembly line, getting draped round fat ones, thin ones, old ones and young ones in turn. The Manager accompanying me was horrified. He kept saying: "Oh, Miss Phoenix, I'm so sorry. Let me get it back for you."

"Oh no you don't! They bought it for me, didn't they?"

Chapter Twenty-Two

The casualties of *Coronation Street* are made all the sadder for its successes. For some tragedy trailed fame like an albatross after a ship of fools. Peter Adamson was one of those casualties. In his fight against booze he has been all the way down to hell and back. Peter admits he was always a heavy drinker but it is my belief that his alcoholism was a result of Len Fairclough. Peter is not aggressive by nature and everywhere he went – especially when he walked into a pub – men would say: "So you're bloody Len Fairclough. Put your fists up."

One drink and another and another made him aggressive enough to cope with it.

Peter was an actor/manager in repertory when he auditioned for the *Street*. He was turned down the first time but called back three months after we went on the air to play a new character – Len Fairclough. Tough, beer-swilling, brawling Len was a target for every member of the public who fancied himself a fighter.

When he thumped Ken Barlow in the Rovers Return, streams of abusive letters poured in calling him a loud-mouthed bully.

Poor Pete even adopted a disguise of flat cap and dark glasses when he went out to get a bit of peace. The weight and responsibility of being a public person took its toll. He turned more and more to the bottle. On screen he remained jovial, lovable Len but in private life the noisy rows, the temper and his loud mouthed public behaviour were killing those of us who knew and loved him. After a slanging match at a fund-raising fete Granada forbade him any more public appearances except for charity. Then they suspended him without pay. For Peter it must have been the bottom.

We all desperately wanted to help but there was nothing we could do. Peter says one of the most difficult things for a drinker to admit is that he *is* an alcoholic. With the help of other alcoholics he began the long fight back. He spent long periods in hospital and when he came back to the *Street* for the first time after his suspension we were all on tenterhooks for him. We waited and waited. A week – two weeks – three weeks. We waited for him to take another drink. But he did not and we know now that he will not. If someone slips him a Mickey Finn – and there are some funny people about – he goes straight outside to be ill.

I can't begin to say how much I love and respect Peter. He is something very, very special is our Pete and always will be. Even when he went through the bad time and he was impossible, quite impossible. But those of us who knew him and knew what he was really like went on loving him through all his terrible moments. And believe me he had some. Peter was drinking heavily all the time. At public appearances, at parties and often in the studio, too. He was told that such was the condition of his liver, if he kept it up he would be dead by forty.

Peter is gutsy enough to tell people about the agony of drying out in hospital in the hope that his experiences will help others similarly afflicted. He works with other alco-

holics in various prisons throughout Britain and spends
time in psychiatric wards where patients who remain mute
for doctors talk freely to him. That is the real Peter
Adamson and for Alan and me he is ten feet tall. Len is still
to be seen swigging ale in the Rovers but these days it isn't
even shandy in that pint pot. When Peter came back after
recovering, he had a line of dialogue to say which to me
shows the guts of the man. It was practically his first line,
and he had to say: "Doctors don't know everything. They
give you pills when a couple of pints would do you more
good."

It is to his eternal credit that he got that line out without
gagging.

Actors can be the cruellest people in the world but at the
same time they can be the most generous, the most warm
and the most sensitive of people when you are in trouble.
And the cast of *Coronation Street* have hearts as big as
whales.

Just a small isolated group were not generous to Peter
but they cannot help being made the way they are. Because
we had known him longer and knew what the man was like
beneath the booze we were more readily understanding.
Perhaps if I had been a stranger coming into the *Street* and
bumping into an incoherent Peter (and I was on the end of
it a lot of the time) I might have thought "I'm not working
with *that*". But for the rest of us he is our Pete and we love
him. One thing I know – and Alan knows it too – if at any
time we were in trouble Peter, our friend, would travel any
distance and move any stone to get us out of it. Can we say,
Peter, dear old mate, the feeling is mutual.

The characters we played in the *Street* inevitably
dominated our lives. With the help of his wife, Jean and
sons, Greig and Michael, Peter learned to live with Len
Fairclough and I suppose you could say he was one of the

lucky ones. Some never learned to live without the protective shell of their *Coronation Street* self once it was taken away from them. And in 1964 the axe fell.

For the first time the show was toppled from its number one spot by the BBC's *Steptoe and Son* and the programme planners decided it was time for changes.

Famous faces found themselves on the dole. Other producers were reluctant to use actors so closely connected in viewers minds as a *Coronation Street* character. We were all wondering who would be the next to go.

Chapter Twenty-Three

Among the first victims of the axe were Ivan Beavis and Doreen Keogh who, as Harry Hewitt and Concepta, had provided the *Street* with its first "wedding". They were on holiday together in Spain and heard the news when they got back. They both found it difficult to get work after leaving the *Street* because they were so strongly identified with their *Coronation Street* roles. Today their careers are thriving and both are regularly seen on television but, at first, they suffered long periods of unemployment.

It was worse for Frank Pemberton, who played Frank Barlow, who was out of the *Street*, too, that year. For him the news was just as sudden and shocking. There are always too many actors chasing too few jobs and, when your face is as familiar as Frank's, the word type-cast begins to haunt. Once he was told bluntly: "We can't use you. As soon as you appear everyone will say, 'Oh, look, it's him from *Coronation Street*'."

Today's audiences, I believe, are more sophisticated, but in those days it was harder. Less than a year after leaving the *Street* he was on the dole. One February day in 1965 he was on his way to the Employment Exchange when a stroke struck him down. Even in his agony someone looked down at him and he heard them say: "Oh, look! It's Mr. Barlow from *Coronation Street*."

He spent months in hospital and when he came out he had lost the use of his left arm and could only walk painfully on crutches.

He was brought back into the *Street* for a while in a wheelchair (at the kind intervention of producer, Harry Kershaw) and although it was a kind-hearted thing to do, it came a little too late. It is a very sad story and I believe it was his departure from *Coronation Street* that helped his stroke along and finally resulted in his death. Ours is a tough profession. Every actor knows that tomorrow it could be their turn for the hard times. It is all in the throw of the dice. Frank's spell in the *Street* was not the comeback he hoped for and when he returned from Manchester it was to the news that his wife wanted a divorce.

I am happy to think that he found some happiness before he died in his marriage to the girl who nursed him in hospital, Sheila Cook. With her he lived in a bungalow in Sussex specially fitted up for his wheelchair. Right up to his death in 1971, he still talked of having "another go" in television.

It was thought by some of us that the death of Martha Longhurst that same year was one of the biggest mistakes ever made. For me it meant the loss of a dear friend from the cast. I had lived with Lynne Carroll, who played Martha, at her house in Blackpool in my struggling rep days.

She and her husband, Bert Palmer, were always so kind to me. But the death knell had tolled for Martha. While Harry and Concepta moved to Ireland and a £5,000 win on "Ernie" for Frank Barlow bought him a house in Cheshire, Martha was killed off, never to return. She had a heart attack in the snug bar of the Rovers at the table she shared with Ena Sharples and Minnie Caldwell. We none of us thought Granada would do it and we were confident Martha would get a last-minute reprieve.

Peter, whose job it was to pronounce her gone, refused to say the line at rehearsals. When the scene was actually being recorded he hesitated, so that his words could be easily cut. For a few deliberate seconds he waited, then said: "She's dead."

He could not believe even then that Granada would let her die and he even bet a fiver on it. He hoped his final line would be edited out and Martha rushed to eventual recovery in hospital.

While Martha was dying the rest of us were supposed to be having a sing-song round the piano, and what a tearful bunch of so-called merrymakers we made. We knew Lynne would not appear again and we knew she did not want to go. We were supposed to be having a good time, but we were just wiping the tears away and doing another take. It was terrible.

There was no signature tune that night. The credits rolled up in silent tribute to Martha as she lay slumped over the table, her spectacles fallen at her side. Viewers wrote a thousand letters regretting her passing, but the departure of Lynne was every bit as poignant as Martha's screen demise.

She said it seemed an age before Peter came out with the line that wrote her out of *Coronation Street* for good.

"Say something, mate, even if it's only goodbye," she kept thinking, through his seconds of silence.

Happily, her husband, Bert, was appearing in the studio next door that night and, as soon as the scene was over, she ran to him and collapsed sobbing in his arms. Bert rescued Martha's hat and glasses from the set where a props boy was clearing up. The kid protested they were needed for next week's credits, but Bert told him: "You're not having these. You'll just have to get another pair."

He gave them to a tearful Lynne and she still has them, along with the cine film Bert took of her "dying" the night the episode was screened.

Even today, people still ask, after many successful appearances in other shows: "Weren't you Martha Longhurst?"

If the scriptwriters had not killed her off she would most likely be soldiering on with the *Street*. I can't help but wonder if death had not been decreed for Martha Longhurst, would life be different for her today?

Chapter Twenty-Four

That was the year a new family came to the *Street*; the Ogdens – Stan, Hilda and their dizzy daughter, Irma. The public fell for Sandra Gough's saucy Irma but stardom for Sandra became an unsettling business. It taught her the tough lesson that sometimes success can be harder to live with than failure. But no matter what one thought about Sandra she was marvellous as Irma and one thing is certain – character-wise the show lost a good deal when she left.

Irma's mum and dad – Stan and Hilda Ogden – proved every bit as popular with the public as their daughter. They loved Bernard Youens for his endearingly shiftless Stan and took Jean Alexander's Hilda – curlers and all – to their hearts. I could always raise a laugh at public appearances by hollering: "I'll knock them bloody curlers right through 'er 'ead one of these days!" They always knew who I meant.

Smartly dressed and pretty, with soft curling hair, Jean Alexander can go almost unrecognised without the turban and curlers; an anonymity, reserved as she is, she must have sometimes welcomed.

It was sad saying goodbye to Arthur Lowe. He was superb as Mr. Swindley of the *Street's* drapery shop but wished for anonymity off-screen. When he left the *Street* in 1965 he adamantly refused to pose for pictures in the character of Mr. Swindley or do anything to perpetrate the role. It was a shrewd move. Some who left the *Street* sank into obscurity. He is now one of the best-known actors on television and in the cinema today. Arthur never ceased to amuse me. He used to play the most awful tricks. We would be standing together waiting to go on set and just before our cue he would tell me some old music hall joke and leave me to face the cameras, shoulders heaving and doing my best to keep my face straight.

We were all prisoners in a way of the characters we created. Jennifer Moss came into the show at fifteen to play ten-year-old Lucille Hewitt. A Wigan schoolgirl when *Coronation Street* was cast, she took a fortnight off school to play the part. Jenny was a slim, slightly built little thing who at first had no trouble in looking six years younger. The trouble began when her bust began to develop. She had to bind it down with tape in order to look her television age. Life was not easy for Jenny. Here she was, growing into a young woman, wanting to smoke and drink like any girl her age, but every time the public saw her doing it, a little bit of illusion was chipped away. More than that. Sometimes they were shocked and horrified because, of course, many did not realise her real age. I suppose I used to mother her a bit in the beginning.

"Jenny," I would lecture her. "You are supposed to be a little girl. Don't smoke in public, don't take drinks in public. The public think you're a kid and that is what you have got to be for them. If you must drink and smoke, don't do it in public."

As the song says, "Poor Jenny, bright as a penny." It

was hard for her. She was earning big money, drove a fast sports car and had plenty of boy-friends; enough to gladden any teenage heart. And here was Phoenix telling her to keep it all to herself – telling her, "Don't let people see you growing up." But Jenny is a girl with a mind of her own. I'm very fond of her. But, as well she knows, when she was a kid I often didn't know whether to give her a kiss or, as they say down *Coronation Street*, "a smack bum".

We were good friends in those days and spent a couple of holidays in Majorca together. She is not a kid any more but a young lady of twenty-six with a daughter of her own, five-year-old Naomi Ruth, and in June, 1974, she left the cast of *Coronation Street* so she could spend more time with Naomi. Jenny had her trials and tribulations growing up as she did in the *Street*. I will always remember her as she looked on her twenty-first birthday at a party for two hundred people. She wore an empire line dress and her hair was entwined with flowers. She looked beautiful.

Minnie Caldwell is probably the one member of *Coronation Street* who has little in common with her creator, Margo Bryant. Whereas Minnie is a dim, dotty old dear, Margo is an elegant, self-possessed, intrepid world traveller with a flair and fondness for Paris hats. And as for being gentle, she will tell you herself she is as tough as old boots. Her pet hate is inefficiency, especially in aeroplanes, where she is known to strike the fear of God into the cabin staff.

Minnie and Margot do share one characteristic. They both love cats. Margot once took tins of cat food by the dozen to Italy and fed them to the abundant, half-starved cat population of Venice. She has owned two cats in the script; both called Bobby. The first died a few years ago and was replaced by Bobby, Mark II. Margot chose the name herself. The scriptwriter had originally called the cat

Skippy. Her own particular furry friend was grandly dubbed the Earl of Hammersmith.

So don't feel sorry for Minnie Caldwell when she's getting the worst of it from Ena. Our Margot is a fine, elegant lady who can give as good as she gets any day of the week. But I swear she really does talk to cats – and what's more, they answer back.

Chapter Twenty-Five

Among the late arrivals to *Coronation Street* were Irene Sutcliffe, who used to play Maggie Clegg, mother of Gordon Clegg, Bill Kenwright in real life. Another of the newer arrivals was Diana Davies who, as Norma Ford, came in as assistant to Maggie in the corner shop. Elsie Tanner was always on good terms with the inhabitants of the corner shop and, strangely enough, Pat Phoenix found three very good friends. Lovely, gentle Irene; Diana, witty, kind, understanding, and Bill Kenwright, great friend and now-adays near-tycoon of the theatre. All three of them made an impact on my life which remains with me today.

And there is lovely Eileen Derbyshire, who plays Emily Nugent, a gentle soul and a superb actress of great range, as anyone who has heard her in her numerous roles in radio plays can testify. Thank God she's got a sense of humour. Aware of the adoration that Margot Bryant and I have for animals, she approached us rather diffidently one morning.

"Knowing how you two feel about this I don't suppose you'll be really interested," she said, twinkling, "but I'd like you to know I'm going to have a baby." We were delighted for her, but teased her unmercifully.

"Oh, I'm so sorry," Margot said, eyebrows raised in sympathy. "What a pity it couldn't have been kittens."

Eileen took it the way it was meant and dissolved into giggles. Happily married to a garage owner, she now has a beautiful little boy whom Margot and I often visit.

Bill Roache, who plays Ken Barlow, and Graham Haberfield, who is the *Street*'s Jerry Booth, are also great personal friends of mine. Bill Roache always, and unwittingly, makes a great impression on the ladies. He almost has them swooning. But a kinder more understanding man I have yet to meet.

I remember on one occasion we were location shooting somewhere in Salford. Those of us who were not working were closeted inside a pub away from the eyes of the general public. A gauche and, sadly, somewhat spotty young girl approached the floor manager in desperation to see Bill Roache. She was so persistent, he finally agreed. However, on sight of Bill, her idol, she was so overcome by excitement she dropped to the floor in an epileptic fit. It was Bill who dropped to his knees on the dusty floor and cradled her in his arms until the shaking stopped. Then he took time out from his brief break to escort her to her home round the corner. That is the Bill Roache I know and love.

Graham Haberfield is the great chef of *Coronation Street*. He loves to cook and we all love his cooking. In fact some of us put on weight by sampling too much of Graham's goodies. Not only does he catch his own fish but knows how to smoke them, too. He once aroused the ire of Granada's car park keeper by assembling his fish smoking outfit on the car park in the middle of the city and busily got to work smoking trout so that his mates in *Coronation Street* could have smoked trout for lunch.

Graham is also a great wag. On one epic occasion on the countdown to transmission, as the floor manager counted down to two, Graham's voice soared across the studio: "Goodbye real world . . ."

They are still saying it today.

Another of the *Street's* wags is Kenneth Farrington, who plays Annie Walker's son. His favourite gambit on the countdown is, "Oh, my God! What's my first line!"

Then, of course, there is dear Brian Mosley, who plays Alf Roberts, with his many children, who delights the cast with his beautifully drawn cartoons, always sending somebody in the *Street* up.

And Stephen Hancock, who plays Ernest Bishop, a fine professional musician and composer. On one occasion I remember Alan and I and friend, Harry Littlewood, went along to see Stephen conduct his own music at a brass band contest. Bernard Youens was to be the compere. The music was to be played by the police band.

Bunny, examining handcuffs backstage in the interval, snapped them round his wrist, to the consternation of the constable. A key could not be found to open them. Bunny did the whole night's compering to a packed house in handcuffs. The audience thought it was a gag, but we knew better. They later had to send to headquarters to get a key to release him.

Neville Buswell, also one of the gang, who plays Ray Langton, spends his spare moments on *Coronation Street* inventing a ridiculous and funny language which has been taken up by the jokers of the cast. Sentences like "You've scrimmed my plinge" – which does not mean a thing – cause concern and bewilderment to onlookers.

And dear Betty Driver, long time friend and dog lover like myself, who was kind and understanding during the days of my mother's illness and who called frequently to see her. She is an incredible lady with two careers. Long before becoming the *Street's* Betty Turpin she was a singer with many of the big and famous bands. She tells a lovely story of her days as a band singer. The occasion was an epic and prodigiously expensive production. Her dress had cost hundreds of pounds. The setting was a curving staircase down which Betty was to float as the band below went into the introduction. Down the stairs, head held high, came Betty in clouds of tulle. Halfway down she tripped and sprawled head first the rest of the way. The band, undeterred, played on and Betty sang her opening line flat out on the floor. What a trouper!

Strangely enough, Betty and I, as children, lived quite close to one another. And my friend, Bill Nadin, actually lived next door to her at one time.

Barbara Mullaney I have also known over the years. Another all rounder – singer, dancer, actress, who, like me, slogged it out through all the lean years of the business. We were brought together again before she joined *Coronation Street* and became Rita Littlewood by our mutual friends Peter Dudley and Ray and Adele Rose. So you see, it really is one big family.

Chapter Twenty-Six

We get all sorts through the post like people's gas bills and mortgages and straightforward requests for money. Not only this, but direct phone calls using phoney identities. The first time it happened to me was on a transmission day, when everyone is rushing around like mad and every second counts, because it is the day we are filming the actual programme. The switchboard, who under normal circumstances would never have interrupted, came through with a call from "my cousin" who had said it was terribly urgent. I thought it must be my cousin Ivy and dashed to the phone.

An Irish voice said: "Elsie, me darlin', you don't know me, but I'm in terrible trouble with my husband. He gave me thirty pounds to pay the rent and I spent it. Now could you possibly lend me thirty pounds?"

I swallowed a Shakespearean oath and, with great restraint in the circumstances, I simply said: "Well, I'm terribly sorry, I wish I had thirty pounds, but I'm in the same boat – broke! Why don't you be honest and tell him you've spent it and if he is a reasonable man it will be all right."

The woman must have been a tremendous actress to get through Granada's watchdog switchboard.

Without the public there is no point in anyone being an actor, and I am happy to give them all the time in the world, except Sunday, and that's mine.

But there are occasions when it is absolutely necessary to be alone. Like, say, when you are dying to go to the loo. It happened to me when I was on holiday in Cornwall with Bill and we had gone out shark fishing with local fishermen. With the boat bouncing about at all angles – Bill up to his neck in gum boots and fish, and me in a fisherman's jersey – and the loo being festooned with fish hooks – I thought I would leave the call of nature until I got ashore with our three-shark catch.

Word had spread through the tiny harbour town that I was on board and, by the time we reached the quayside, a crowd had gathered with autograph books. It took longer than I thought to come alongside and, by this time, my urge had become a dire necessity.

"Will you just let me through. I'm going over there and I'll be right back, I promise."

But one very determined lady said: "You'll sign this before you go," and shoved an autograph book under my nose. There was nothing for it but to push past her and, as I did, I heard her say: "Who wants her bloody autograph, anyway."

Bill remarked, "She wasn't near enough to the quayside, or I would have pushed her in."

Using the loo has become less of a private affair for me – more of a public adventure. I had been shopping in a large department store and faced a long drive home.

"Nothing for it, Phoenix," I told myself. "You'll just have to dash in and hope you go unnoticed." Scarf around my head and face averted I nipped through the washroom, pushed my penny in the door and gained the inner sanctum with a sigh of relief. Alone at last!

Then, from over the partition, a hand appeared waving a piece of paper. The hand was followed by an arm and the arm by a head. She must have been standing on the next door loo seat. I gazed upwards, astounded. The woman met my startled stare calmly.

"Can I have your autograph?" she said.

Holidays are essential in our pace-making business — time to relax. But it does not always work out that way. After one hell of a season, overworked and overtired, all I wanted to do was lie on some sunny beach. I grabbed the first jet to the Canary Islands. On my first day there, stretched out on a beach bed, eyes closed, blissfully oblivious to the world around me, a heavy hand was suddenly plonked on my bare midriff and a voice bellowed: "Elsie Tanner! You didn't mind us waking you, did you?"

I opened my resigned eyes to see two perfectly strange ladies and said, "No. I don't mind. Only next time don't jump on my stomach — try whispering in my ear."

The best rest I ever had was when I set sail on a banana boat with a group of old age pensioners. I had been ill; I wanted to get away on my own and the only boat I could get a berth on was bound for Tenerife with twenty senior citizens. They were a super bunch and I had a marvellous time.

The Tunisian island of Djerba where I spent a holiday with Bill and Gordon Warburton and his wife, Elsa, is a finger of sand in the middle of the Mediterranean consisting of not much more besides two hotels, a couple of little Arab villages and miles and miles of empty golden beaches.

Walking the deserted beach one day I saw three beautiful, bronzed nude ladies sporting themselves in the water; their voices carried clearly over the waves. They were

German – two younger girls and a middle-aged woman. With their blonde hair and tanned gold skin they looked like Rhine maidens. They beckoned to me like the lorelei and, like the sailors of old, I could not resist. Pulling off my shirt and jeans as I ran towards the water's edge, I fell naked as they were into the spray. There was no English spoken but a union of laughter was formed between strangers that met in the sea.

That night at dinner a murmur buzzed round the tables; heads turned towards the door. The cause of the excitement was the entrance of my three Rhine maidens. I caught the eye of the senior maiden as the waiters ushered them deferentially to a table. She nodded in polite, though austere, recognition.

"Who is that lady?" I asked a waiter curiously.

His answer stunned me. I never did find out who the young girls were but I was told they may have been nieces. But the now fully dressed and slightly forbidding lady with whom I had frolicked naked in the sea was none other than the widow of Hitler's Luftwaffe chief, Herman Goering.

One of my most recent holidays was spent on the island of Malta. I had never been there. "In that case", said Alan, "let's go".

The trouble was it was short notice and we had no accommodation. Friend, Joan Dean, said: "But you must go and stay with Mo. He'd be delighted to have you."

Mo being a magnificent Maltese hotelier of our acquaintance – in appearance a mixture of Spencer Tracey, James Cagney and George Raft with the charm of manner to delight anyone.

"You come," hollered Mo, over the phone. "I will find room. You will be my guests."

So that is how we came to have one of the happiest holidays ever at Mo's Golden Sands Hotel with its huge swimming pool, lifts to the beach and its delightfully informal family atmosphere. And Mine Host himself, the delightful all-embracing Mo Fenech.

We did everything. We were in time for the Festival of Malta. Mo saw to it that we had grandstand seats. We did the night clubs, the restaurants, and all day we lounged around the swimming pool, making friends with people from all over England who still remain our friends today. Alan became involved in a football match – Guests v Hotel Staff.

Now, the staff's idea of a football pitch was a rock strewn granite square. I had vague forebodings. I did not want to see Alan get hurt but, sure enough, he did. He was not the only casualty. Several English guests sprained ankles and ricked shoulders. Alan, however, had torn a ligament. He was hobbling about for two and a half months after that but when we returned to England he was happy to know that his mate, footballer Georgie Best, was suffering from the same complaint. They sat playing poker together, wounded legs in the air.

But despite that, Malta was a dream holiday We took out a boat with two English friends. The hold was stuffed with goodies and several large bottles of Pimms Number Six (my favourite tipple). We cruised the islands, stopping off to swim and sunbathe, cutting engines and drifting on the waves, then roared back into port, slightly squiffed. Had we been on the roads we would have been done for drunken driving.

One day, when we get a break, we'll go back.

Chapter Twenty-Seven

I had some notoriety as a firebrand at Granada. I became in a way the cast's unofficial shop steward, though some might say I was just a damned nuisance. If something was amiss on the fourth floor, I felt it was the duty of those on the fifth to put it right – scripts, personal problems, illness and so forth. If there was anything wrong or if everybody was getting upset, it was always an excuse for me to go upstairs and let fly. If there was some injustice or somebody was suffering over something, I believed "upstairs" ought to know about it and I – mounted on my white charger – would tell them. Power to their elbow, they occasionally listened to me. Who could help it when I was blasting off? I think they enjoyed it, to tell the truth.

"You've had it too quiet for a fortnight," I would grin at whoever was occupying the executive suite.

"Now, what can we have a row about."

Once it was trying to get them to put divans in our dressing rooms – standard furnishings in any type of screen or stage star dressing rooms where artists might wait for hours before they are called to work. One of the girls said:

"I think they are bothered about us locking ourselves in with the fellows and having some hanky panky."

"You don't need divans to do that," I said.

"Listen," I said to H.V.K. (an affectionate term for producer Harry V. Kershaw) who was the nearest available ear and usually the one to suffer from my explosions, "What about divans in our dressing rooms? We spend hours in there waiting and there is simply nowhere to put our feet up." I threatened to bring a camp bed and lie down in the corridor. Harry K. went to work and we got the divans.

Harry Kershaw is a great friend. If I needed advice and Alan wasn't around to give it, I would go to Harry. Because he does it with kindness. His success in *Coronation Street* I think was first because he was a human being. The personalities in *Coronation Street* matter to him as people. I think he tried at times to be ruthless, but I don't think Harry was ever really successful at being ruthless. He would sometimes pretend to me, but somehow the kindness shone through. He is a man of great integrity with his own set of rules which he has kept all his life.

When the scriptwriters had written something which I considered too soft for Elsie to say like "those poor starving little children" instead of "them poor kids", I would tell them: "It's schmaltzy. I know Elsie and whatever *you* think, you can't have her saying that." They would gently pat the head of their idiot child and, more times than not, humour me by changing the line. But only if I was right and never, ever if I was wrong. This applied to any of us on *Coronation Street* who complained about scripts.

After the divans they gave us two Green Rooms. That is what actors call rest rooms. Half the cast use one and half the other. The card players like Bill Roache, Graham Haberfield, Neville Buswell, Brian Moseley, Stephen

Hancock, Irene Sutcliffe, Doris Speed, Jenny Moss and Jack Howarth, the much loved Diana Davies and mate Peter Adamson, not to mention A. Browning and Bunny Youens, would congregate in one. The girls would go in the other for a natter. Betty Driver, Barbara Mullaney, Julie Goodyear, Margot Bryant, Eileen Derbyshire, Jean Alexander and Violet Carson could usually be found in there. I don't play poker and I considered I had nothing to offer in the way of conversation, so I could usually be found up at the other end with a book in my hand or watching the scenes rehearsed and shot.

I liked to watch scenes taking shape. *Coronation Street* actors in action are quite special to my mind. I would pop in and out of both Green Rooms for the odd half-hour's chat, but most of the day I liked to sit, glancing over my lines or reading. I used to get through five novels a week. Eric Prytherch, our Welsh producer, nicknamed Taffy, thought I spent more time reading than learning my lines.

"Don't worry, Taff," I once told him. "By Thursday I'll be able to say them backwards."

"You usually do," he shot back.

I hear that after I left the show, Julie Goodyear, who plays barmaid Bet Lynch, said and did a rather touching thing. It was bitterly cold weather and she noticed that the name of one of the older members of the cast, who had been a bit under the weather, was up on the list for an outside scene. Outside scenes are shot in an old railway siding at the back of Granada. It's a sort of old shed and we call it "the street where the sun never shines". On the hottest day it is cold in that street. It is surrounded by walls, it is damp and the brickwork is rotting because it has been standing for so long.

We have no stand-ins and there is a sort of draughty hut – never very warm. It is death out there on a cold day. And it always seems to happen that an artist has six or seven outside shots to do on the run.

They tell me Julie saw this particular artist's name on the list and said: "Have they gone daft up there? I know what Pat would do. I'm going up there to play little hell."

Well, she did go upstairs, and the artist's name was taken off the list. No one had meant to be unkind or heartless. They simply had not noticed. And that is why an unofficial shop steward can sometimes work wonders. I am sure it was the gentle consideration of H.V.K. that helped to keep the cast working so tightly together.

For instance, on hot days in the studio (which can be unbearable) he always made sure there was iced orange juice to cool everybody down.

Julie and I share a joke which stems from when she first came into the show. She always says she owes her chance in show business and in *Coronation Street* to me; which is sweet of her, but all I ever did was advise her to get some experience in rep, which she did, and developed into the actress she is today. One day on set during rehearsal, someone was bitching about not being able to sit down in the chair as the script directed because another artist was mistakenly already sitting there.

It was a silly little argument over nothing, of the kind which arises when people are working as closely together as our lot. On *Coronation Street* we very seldom did retakes because of mistakes by actors, but only if the boom got in the way or for some other technical hitch. The time element is tight, and it is very like giving a live performance. It is a strain on the actors and technicians alike and, on transmission day, all our nerves are stretched a bit tight.

Discussing the incident with Julie afterwards I propounded my theory that one should always say "my fault" whether it is or isn't.

"The way to do it," I lectured, "is to say 'I'm in the wrong place, aren't I? I'm sure I must be because you are bound to be right.' And if somebody dries up say, 'Oh, it's me. I've gone again.' Always say 'my fault'. It makes for less nervous tension."

The next day, right in the middle of a very tense and difficult scene for me, one of the carpenters dropped a large hammer from a very great height. It fell with a resounding crash, completely drowning my words. In the seconds of silence which followed, Julie's voice carolled across the set.

"My fault!" she sang out.

After that, whenever anything went wrong, Julie and I would sing out in unison: "My fault!"

It was Doris Speed who was responsible for "My Falk" as it became known on the *Street*. I'm a great fan of Peter Falk's *Columbo* and as Doris and I were rehearsing a scene together I was chatting away about his technique.

"He never looks directly at the camera," I enthused. He plays every scene with his back half-turned; he seems always to play slightly off camera."

"How do you mean," queried Doris.

"I'll show you when we do this next bit," says I.

"Action" came the call and went into the scene.

"Now, look, Mrs. Walker, it's like this . . ." I began my impression of Peter Falk – picking at a cigarette packet, hunching away from the camera, rubbing my nose, gazing vaguely around, playing it for all I was worth. Doris smiled away at me. The scene ended.

"That was a take," someone said.

I could not believe it. I thought we were just running through the scene to time it.

"No, no, you can't," I pleaded.

Everybody, especially Doris who had known it was a take, was falling about. It was only five seconds but I adamantly refused to watch it the night it was screened. And I wouldn't let Alan watch it, either. It became a gag in the *Street* whenever I stumbled over a line they'd say: "Pat is doing her 'Peter Falk'."

We are very much a family at Granada. We even tend to go to the same clubs and pubs although as most of my professional life is spent in going out, I like to spend my time of relaxation staying in. The one place I like to go is the Film Exchange Club in Manchester, two minutes from Granada, where one is gently ministered to by Patrick and his crew, who understand all about the stresses and strains of artists and writers in television. The steak is succulent, the shrimps are savoury and the champagne is always cold. See you soon, Patrick.

Chapter Twenty-Eight

As the faces of *Coronation Street* became more famous, so the rumours about those faces became more fantastic. One of the lads would only have to be involved in a car accident after a night out for it to make headlines. The simplest court case involving one of us escalated to almost criminal proportions. Philip Lowrie, who played my son Dennis, was once up on a simple speeding charge.

"It's Elsie Tanner's son," whispered the Clerk of the Court to the Magistrate.

It didn't help Philip. He was still fined £7.50.

Philip and I were the victims of a most fantastic rumour that seemed to gather momentum as it went along. The story went round, and even got into the newspapers, that we were engaged to be married. Now Philip and I were very fond of each other but to talk of marriage was just nonsense. I thought of him as a son and I am sure he thought of me as much as a mother as anything else. We were, to be sure, great mates, but that was most definitely all.

In a way, I suppose, I was partially to blame for the misunderstanding that arose. I was talking to a couple of reporters one day who asked if I was fond of Philip. I said, the way theatrical people do, "Of course, I love Philip. I have a very deep affection for him."

Later that evening the Press telephoned and asked if I was engaged. I was flabbergasted. "Why do you think that?" I said. It seemed my talk of "love" and "affection" had been seriously misconstrued, and the next remark confirmed it.

"Well, this sort of thing happens more abroad," he said.

"What sort of thing?" I asked bleakly.

"An older woman marrying a younger man," he said.

"Just a minute, sonny," I said. "Before you go any further, that's not what we're talking about. We are talking about being fond of each other, of being mates."

"But you used the word 'love'," he insisted.

"*All* actors use the word 'love'," I said, and hung up.

Somehow or other the story about an engagement appeared the next day. When anyone rang to ask if I was engaged I said: "Sure, I am. I can't make up my mind if it's a tall thin Welshman or a short fat Scotsman."

But one way or another there seemed to be a determined effort to engage me to Philip. I suppose, once again, it was my fault. I wore a ring he gave me on my engagement finger, the only one it fitted, and it was noticed by a reporter.

"Are you engaged?" came the question again. "Who gave you the ring?"

"No, I'm not engaged. Philip Lowrie gave me the ring," I said, somewhat foolishly.

That set the whole ball rolling. Poor Philip was in Tasmania and was completely puzzled to get phone calls from England asking, once again, about our "engagement".

I must admit the fault is often mine. I make these tongue

in cheek remarks only to find later I have been taken seriously. Once in Australia on a hectic public appearance, my hands were being clutched from both sides. One arm disappeared into the crush and came back ringless. Someone had taken the opportunity to slip the ring from my finger and I didn't even feel it.

The Press got hold of the story and one very slow reporter rang me up. I could almost see him laboriously writing down everything I said. He asked me what sort of ring it was. I told him an amethyst.

"Was it gold?" he asked.

"No, you bloody fool. It was brass," I retorted. And that is how he described it. "A brass bound amethyst", read his report the next day.

I am on the best of terms with most of the Press and over the years have come to number many of them among my close personal friends. It is in part to Keith McDonald of the *Manchester Evening News* I owe the idea of writing this book. It was he who first encouraged me to begin an autobiography. He has written much about me over the years, *most* of it nice and *all* of it accurate.

One thing that really makes me mad is when a reporter comes to meet the actors of *Coronation Street* without bothering to learn their real names. I gave one very young reporter what I believe to be the lesson of his life when he came along to interview us one afternoon. Not only did he not know our proper names but he kept addressing us by the names of the characters we played.

"Listen," I said sweetly, "I think I should take you round and introduce you to everybody.

"This is Dame Sybil Thorndike, and this is Dame Edith Evans and this is John Barrymore . . ."

He wrote them all down carefully.

I was tempted to let him go away happy in his ignorance

and get a roasting from his editor but, at the last minute, just as he was leaving, I called him back.

"Look sonny," I told him. "Don't take any notice of those names. Next time you go along to talk to people just find out what their names are beforehand." I gave him the right names.

It is fair to say that by and large the Press have treated me well, and apart from the stories on Philip, most of what they have written about me is accurate enough. I missed Philip when he left the *Street* in 1968, but it was right for him to go. He wanted to try his hand at something else. He was not long out of drama school when he auditioned for the *Street* and was one of the original cast. He left after a year to work in the theatre and Granada was inundated with letters from viewers who wanted him back. After a year he returned and spent another seven years with the *Street* and I suppose he thought eight years as Dennis Tanner was quite enough.

Chapter Twenty-Nine

Coronation Street proved the tops down under. The show stormed Australian television in 1963 and by 1966 it was popularity plus. Time, it was decided, to give the Aussies a glimpse of the real thing. Doris Speed, Arthur Leslie, H.V.K. and me were chosen to be the *Street's* ambassadors. None other than the Prime Minister, Mr. Harold Wilson, proposed to wish goodbye to Jack and Annie Walker and Elsie Tanner from Number Ten Downing Street.

I'm a Labour Party supporter and so is Doris and a speaking acquaintance of Harold Wilson's whom I have met at various party rallies, and the trip to Number Ten was sent up something rotten. We were joking and laughing on the way there with utterances like: "I wonder who stones the steps"; "There's bound to be an outside lavvy"; and "Do they shoot you if you don't wipe your feet". We were still in a skittish mood when we lifted the knocker at Number Ten. But before it banged down the door opened and we were ushered down a long red carpeted corridor.

It was like a posh funeral parlour and suddenly we all became terribly nervous. Not of seeing Harold, because I had met him several times before, but at the thought of the

great who had trod these halls before us. Here were we, the
denizens of a fictitious back street in Salford, following in
austere and majestic footsteps.

Suddenly there were whisperings to the left and right of
us as we tripped dutifully down the corridor. Curtains were
lifted and faces peeped out. We were shown solemnly into a
hushed ante-room where we waited, knees knocking and all
levity gone. When the door opened and we were shown
through to where Harold waited, I was so relieved to see
him that I threw my arms round him.

"Are you all right?" he asked in some alarm.

"Oh, phew! Out there!" I stammered.

"Come on, sit down," he said, and led me to a small sofa.
Then he said: "You know, I've never seen anything like it.
We've had everybody in this place but no one has aroused as
much curiosity and comment among the staff as you
have."

We sat sipping sherry and talking about acting, politics,
cabbages and kings. Jim Callaghan was there, we met Mrs.
Wilson, saw the herb garden and took a walk around. It
was a marvellous afternoon. Some might be blasé about it
but to us it was another accolade and we loved it. Although
Harry did mutter in the taxi going back: "I do wish these
pipe smokers would remember that other people smoke
cigarettes," chucking his last empty packet through the
window.

He had spent the whole afternoon stepping over legs,
and the particularly long ones of Jim Callaghan, keeping
me supplied for my interminable chain-smoking.

As we left, the Press had gathered in a body outside
Number Ten. Jim draped an arm affectionately over my
shoulder for the benefit of the cameras and the reporters
and said: "I think she's the sexiest thing on television."

The Press had a field day with that remark. There were

cartoons, articles, pictures and even a lampoon on the cover of *Private Eye*.

Our arrival in Adelaide, Australia, was every bit as overwhelming as the send-off had been. Doris and Arthur sedately side by side and me sitting on the back of the car with my feet on the seat. Ticker tape by the bucket-full showered out of windows over public, police and the open-mouthed visitors from *Coronation Street*. Crowds of fifty-thousand plus turned out to see us wherever we went. My impression of that visit is people, people everywhere. Thousands of them lining every street. At one point Doris, Harry, Arthur and I had to visit a doctor for treatment for arms swollen with too much handshaking, and backs aching from too many affectionate and enthusiastic pats. The Press went berserk and banner headlines screamed: "Never send the Queen to Australia at the same time as *Coronation Street*."

We thought that one would get us incarcerated in the Tower of London when we returned.

Everywhere we moved police cars and motor-cycle outriders accompanied us. One rare free night in Melbourne I decided to sneak off alone to the cinema. Sneak off! I must have been joking. I just got my nose outside the hotel door when sirens screamed and my personal motor-cycle escort zoomed up.

"What's up?" I said. "Where's the fire?"

"We've been instructed to escort you to wherever you wish to go, Miss Phoenix," they said eagerly.

"But I'm only going to the pictures," I said, "and you can't bring your bikes in there. No go home, there's good lads."

But there was no shaking them. I walked the hundred or so yards up the road to the cinema and my two boy scouts did their best to walk their bikes alongside.

When I got back to the hotel Doris, Harry and Arthur were in a panic to know where I had been.

"To the pictures, of course, with my personal outriders," I said grandly, and swept upstairs to bed.

Looking back, my motor-bike knight errants were probably right. I did need protection of a sort. One evening I arranged to meet Arthur, Doris and Harry in the bar of the hotel where we were staying. For the life of me I can't remember if it was Adelaide or Melbourne. But there I was all dressed up like a dog's dinner in my black lace and walking into the bar alone.

I was a bit early so I sat at a table by myself drinking a tomato juice. Two very handsome looking fellows at the bar looked across at me and smiled and little Miss Happy Face gives out with a big hello.

"Ho, ho," I thought. "Fame at last. I'm recognised."

They raised their glasses and I raised mine. A few moments later the bartender appeared at my elbow.

"The gentlemen would like to know if you would join them," he said.

I told him no, thank you, that I was waiting for someone and in any case I did not drink. At that they came over and pleaded with me to have a drink with them. So persuasive were they that I relented and joined them at the bar. One of them began to get very friendly; a little too outgoing, and I began to think he was more than a bit forward when suddenly he leaned over and said: "My room number is 202."

The bartender, hovering, seemed to get a hot flush and an acute case of agitation. He leaned across and in a voice choking with something or other (it may have been gin and tonic) said: "Sir, you are making a great mistake."

"Whadya talking about," said my new friend, aggressively.

I looked goggle-eyed from one to the other, thinking that if the fellow was kind enough to invite me to a party in his room the barman need not get so funny about it. Just then I turned to see if Doris and Arthur had arrived and in a mirror behind me I saw the reflection of the barman holding up an evening paper.

I knew what those banner headlines screamed. "*Coronation Street* takes the town by storm." The whole of the front page was taken up with a picture of Doris, Arthur, H.V.K. and me on a balcony looking out over the city and a sea of upturned faces. The barman was jabbing a finger at it and at the back of my head desperately. I turned to see incredulity then horror cross the faces of my gentlemen friends. It transpired that they had been out in the bush, out of sight and sound of television for years, and this was their first trip to town. They had never seen or heard of Elsie Tanner or *Coronation Street*. I had found the only two Aussies in the country who didn't know me.

"Ma'am," they began, immediately making me feel eighty-nine. "We can't say how sorry we are."

"Don't apologise," I cut in, "I was flattered out of my mind."

One night in Sydney we were invited to see the sights and included in the itinerary was a visit to a famous striptease club.

"Gags, glitter and girls," it announced in oscillating lights outside the club. Dear old Arthur declined on the grounds when you've seen one you've seen 'em all and went off home to have a good night's sleep, leaving Doris, Harry, Norman Frisby, Granada's Press Officer, and the PRO from a local television station. For myself, I felt a bit like Arthur but Doris was undeterred and determined to spend an evening seeing the sights. I was a little worried. What sort of strip show were we going to see? Would she be shocked?

On came the girls. Bare, bewitching and bosomy, gyrating, twisting, swaying, turning. Doris sat impassively at her ringside seat, sipping a dry martini. Then on came the tassel dancer. Bumps and grinds were to say the very least as the tassels swung in every direction. Doris clasped my arm and indicated through the blaring rock music for me to lean towards her so she could whisper above the noise. This is it, I thought. She's shocked. She wants to go home. I could not have been more wrong.

"I do wish," murmured Doris in my ear, ignoring all the obvious attributes of the dancer, "that she wouldn't wear that pale pink lipstick."

After three hectic weeks in Australia it was nice to get away to a place where we could walk down the street without stopping the traffic. That was San Francisco, where not a living soul or hippy knew us. *Coronation Street* had not then been shown on American television and we were free to go about as we pleased. We did the whole tourist bit including a visit to the Redwood Forest where we lunched in a log cabin in the trees.

The barman, a very friendly fellow who looked like Yul Brynner and was playing it for all it was worth, insisted on paying for the drinks I had ordered. Having summed me up correctly as a tourist he looked across to where Doris and Arthur were sitting quietly in a corner and asked: "Who are those people?"

"Just friends," I said vaguely.

How could I explain he was looking at the two most famous publicans in the British Isles.

"In that case you don't have to leave with them," he leered. "Why don't ya stick around, babe."

"Cracked it again, kid," I told myself ruefully. Me and

my big smile! When he started talking about spare bunks in the ranch house I grabbed Doris and Arthur – who were quickly followed by H.V.K. and Norman Frisby – and ran.

"You could have kept him talking 'til I had finished my Manhattan cocktail," said Doris wistfully. I must admit we had fun being anonymous for a change.

San Francisco was beautiful and whatever has happened to us since, it will always remain the most beautiful city in the world to me. Like Tony Bennett I, too, left my heart in San Francisco, if you know what I mean.

America did not see *Coronation Street* until 1972, although they had considered showing the series there the year of our visit. It was felt the show was too downbeat for American taste with a cast of losers. Instead they decided to make their own series about life in a small town. They called it *Peyton Place* and it turned out to be one of America's all-time hits.

Later, when their show was firmly established in the top spot, the cast sent us a photograph of themselves inscribed: "To the Number One show from the Number One show."

The cast of *Peyton Place*, with their faultless radiant features, well-cut clothes and carefully coiffured hair presented a picture of health and prosperity.

We were going to pose for a photograph to send back but the thought of Ena Sharples, Minnie Caldwell, Elsie Tanner and the rest of our crowd standing on the *Coronation Street* cobbles or somewhere in Salford did not seem to be the answer. Some sardonic wag said: "You can't do that. They will think it's a charity appeal."

Chapter Thirty

The saga of a sooty back street in Salford is hardly the stuff
that world hits are made of. But, improbably enough,
Coronation Street was a success from Sierra Leone to
Singapore. Heart is heart in any language, it seems.

It is easy to understand its success in Australia and New
Zealand, but its fans were not only emigrees from the home
country. Native-born Australians and New Zealanders
viewed just as avidly. The cast of *Coronation Street* were
much in demand. Arthur Leslie was asked to open a New
Zealand agricultural show by radio telephone and Violet
Carson also went on the line from her Blackpool home to
open an appeal to raise funds to build a museum. Her
appeal was broadcast on New Zealand radio. Violet's hair-
net was also much in demand there. She gave them one to
be auctioned for charity. It cost about a shilling and fetched
£100.

When I was in Australia someone made a bid for me! I
was being taken round the five real-life Coronation Streets
of Melbourne when a man leaped out at me with an
enormous bunch of flowers and a marriage proposal. All I
could say was: "This is so sudden."

Well, it was.

Wherever you go in Australia you see a different part of the series. Some cities are years behind and others are catching up fast with daily showings. It is from New Zealand that we get the most fanmail and four years in a row it was voted the most popular show on television. But it was the Australians who chartered a plane to come and see us. Over a hundred of them clubbed together for a round-the-world jet flight and they all agreed without a visit to *Coronation Street* the trip would not be worth while. They came and we gave them a party on set.

In Greece and Gibraltar the series started late and English visitors crowded round television sets in hotel lounges and cafes whenever it was broadcast. They said watching vintage episodes was like stepping back in time. Canada was just as enthusiastic, although some of the native-born Canadians were puzzled, not so much by the Lancashire accents but by the Lancashire expressions. A radio programme devoted to the *Street* where listeners could phone in questions resulted in the twenty lines to the station being jammed.

In Holland the programme was enormously popular, especially with students of the English language, but teachers were troubled with students whose pronunciation owed more to Oxford Road, Manchester, than Oxford University. One student wrote to me and said he enjoyed the programme very much but could not understand all the expressions. I began to compile a glossary.

Love (Luv)	Warmer than darling
Lovey (Luvey)	Closer than dear
Chuck or Chucky	Literally a variation of chicken, also a Lancashire endearment
Duck (Ducky)	Similar term of endearment

A chucky egg for brekker	A chicken's egg for breakfast
Clout	To strike, i.e. a clout around the ear 'ole (a punch round the ear)
Niggling	Small irritation, usually of a mental kind or – to nag
Me snap tin	My lunch tin. Snap is food eaten in a work break, usually sandwiches carried to work in a tin
Yer grotty article	Someone not very nice. Grotty (unpleasant)
Mither, Mithered, Mithering	To be bothered, to nag or moan. To persist in irritating
Lady Muck	Satirical reference to female snobbishness, e.g. She thinks she's Lady Muck
To natter	To preach, to talk a lot
Flamin'	Mild oath
A belter	Something good, e.g. A good-looking girl is a belter
Butties	Bread with sommat between it

I don't suppose this helped my Dutch student to pass his English exams but if he ever came to Salford it would take him a lot further than his school books.

Our number one fan had to be a Dutch schoolgirl called Willi Van As. She sent us an intricate scaled model of the *Street* she made herself. She had carefully scrutinised the outside shots and every detail was perfect, except for one. Her pillar box was green like those in Holland. She had, of course, been watching in black and white.

It was not only foreign schoolchildren who found *Coronation Street* instructive. A Lancashire school set up a replica of the *Street*'s Corner Shop where the children bought groceries to help them work out their sums. Grown-ups as well as children have used the *Street* to learn. A Manchester bank installed computers and invited bank accounts for characters from the *Street* to help train their staff to operate it. I bet you anything Elsie Tanner was overdrawn!

In Singapore and Thailand British servicemen and their families found the *Street* a link with home and even the Chinese loved it. But the rickshaw boys of Hong Kong were not so keen. When the programme was on there (with Cantonese subtitles shown vertically) the streets were virtually empty and they did no trade. Even the West Indian islands of Trinidad, Tobago and Barbados ran the programme. In Sierra Leone it was a hot favourite, even if the country did only have three thousand television sets.

It came as no surprise to any of us that when the British Government's Information Services wanted an excerpt from a British television programme to send to African stations, they chose *Coronation Street*.

Chapter Thirty-One

Wedding bells rang for Elsie Tanner in 1967. The bride-groom was her American boy-friend Steve Tanner. And what a wedding! It stretched over two episodes and they were so popular Granada repeated them a few weeks later. Women even wrote to me and said they had bought new hats and had their hair done to sit in their own front rooms and watch the ceremony. Wedding gifts for the happy pair showered in, from tea cosies knitted by old ladies to cheques which we sent to charity. Over a million souvenir programmes of the occasion were sold.

Barbara Cartland wrote an open letter in a magazine advising me how to keep my new husband happy.

There were many who were disappointed that I wasn't marrying my old flame, Len Fairclough. One viewer expressed vitriolic disappointment in a series of disturbing letters. How dare I marry a Yank? The letters came in at an ever-increasing rate to everyone concerned. To me, to Paul and to the then producer, Jack Rosenthal. Then came threats to knife us as we left the studios and it was felt the time had come to inform the police. All the letters were from one person. It all got a bit tense. Jack Rosenthal released the tension one morning when he got a particularly nasty letter describing in detail the punishment that was in store for him if he let the marriage continue.

He stood in the middle of the room, letter in hand, and read it out loud, grinning lopsidedly and punctuating the text with:

"Yes, I'd like that."

"Yes, I'll have that done to me."

"No. I don't fancy that bit."

"No. I'm not having that."

"Yes. I might enjoy that."

We were falling about in hysterics and it did a lot to lighten the atmosphere.

The "wedding" took place in St. Stephen's Methodist Church with Paul Maxwell, as American Steve Tanner, in a US Air Force uniform and me in a knee-length dress of beige satin and lace. The script had us flying off for a honeymoon in Lisbon. In reality I took off for two weeks' well-deserved rest after all the hullabaloo of the wedding.

It was no accident that Steve and Elsie shared the surname Tanner. He was not destined to be around long. In September, 1968, their marriage on the rocks, Steve returned to Coronation Street to see Elsie. He was killed, suspected murdered, falling down a flight of stairs, leaving widowed Elsie free to be her old man-chasing self again.

But her marriage to Steve Tanner left its mark. People have accused me of changing Elsie over the years but it was time, not me, that changed her. She became more aware, more intelligent. When the script gave her affairs of more import and she married the American, she had to be *more* intelligent. The scriptwriters began to give her words of more than one syllable; she began to say things like "psychological". Thirteen years ago she could have been as thick as a plank but today she has progressed because

All My Burning Bridges | 175

people have. Those who live in back-to-back houses these days have cars and their houses are beautifully done-up. They know more about life and more about living. When people accuse me of changing Elsie Tanner I tell them it is not only me, but time, society and they, themselves, that have changed.

Even Elsie's style of dressing has altered. It has had to. Producer Harry Kershaw used to ask me: "Where are all those low-cut satin blouses you used to find for Elsie?"

"*You* go into a shop and try to find satin blouses, tight skirts and stiletto heels, Harry," I would tell him. "You just can't buy them any more."

Tarts these days wear smocks, leather raincoats and platform soles; suitable neither for the old nor the new Elsie.

I have always chosen Elsie's clothes myself, buying them at street markets, little corner shops and multiple stores; places where Elsie would shop. Sometimes I converted something of my own that I'd had for years. Elsie's clothes had to be a bit over the top but people would write in asking for patterns or the names of the shops where I had bought them and say "how very smart". I began to realise that I had another function. People wanted to see me nicely dressed and wanted cheap but nice clothes. I kept well within a budget. I used to get smashing things for £7 and £10 once upon a time. When Elsie married Steve Tanner her taste improved a bit but she still made the odd mistake.

There is one thing television does for a woman. If you see yourself on it for any length of time you do eventually lose all vanity, if you are honest and watch yourself – well you do, if you are me. You see yourself walking away and you see every angle; angles you have never seen before. And I have seen some pretty grotesque angles of me! There were some episodes at the time of my break-up with Steve Tanner where I was supposed to be looking very grotty.

They wiped the make-up off my face, shoved glycerine all over it and greased up my hair. Most of the time I wore a dirty old slip. The house made you sick to look at — piles of ash trays and gin bottles. It went on for some time and if you watch yourself like that week after week you soon find out what you are all about. And I still say the most devastating thing for any actress on television is to watch herself walking away. I guarantee you won't ever have seen that behind wag that way before.

Television cameras are cruel, but like a mirror, they can be your best friend and tell you the truth. There should be no question of self-deception. A mirror should be in the cruellest, hardest light available. Everything is wrong with my face but I still wouldn't change it. I've got a big nose and if I were eighteen today, I might have been tempted to have it bobbed in the fashion of many actresses — but I am so glad I didn't. If nothing else I like to think at least my mug has got a little character.

Basically I am a very plain lady. I am not fishing for compliments. I am being critically honest. On off days my mirror speaks: "My God, Phoenix. What a mess you are."

But my advice to any woman who thinks like me is, Attack! Make the most of what you have got. I think of my face as a very good canvas. Blank — but good for painting on. Two pounds of pollyfilla and one of cement, some mascara and lipstick and it is all stations go and look out world!

Chapter Thirty-Two

If there was one person who relished my success on *Coronation Street* more than any other, it was my mother. Not that she ever told me to my face. She loved watching me on television and when I asked her: "Did you like me in that, Mother? What did you think of it?"

She would more than likely reply:; "Oh, you were all right. But you look so fat." Didn't believe in flattery – my mother.

When I told her that I based my performance as Elsie Tanner on her, she was most indignant.

"I beg your pardon," she said icily, drawing herself up and flashing me a haughty look, "*I* was never a tart."

But nevertheless there was a great deal of my mother in Elsie. The warmth, the love, the way she was everybody's mother. There was a loving toughness about Elsie that came direct from my mother. When she said to Dennis: "Do that again and I'll clout you round the ear 'ole," she was really saying: "Please don't do that. You're breaking my heart."

That is how my mother was with me. Never a compliment to my face but just let anyone else say a word against me. She would defend me with her dying breath. To other people I was "Saint Patricia". To me – "A devil. A friend. A one-woman revolution" – nevertheless, there was always love and support.

In my early days in rep when I didn't care if I worked a fortnight for three pounds, the relatives would say to her: "Why don't you put her in a nice job. She's got her school certificate. Why do you let her roam the country like that for peanuts?"

But my mother would say: "She'll do what she wants to do," and send me a few pounds she could ill afford.

A cousin once said to me: "She would take food from a starving man's mouth to feed you."

I will always be glad she saw the good times with me. When it all started to happen no one was more excited or delighted than she was.

She came on personal appearances with me; her slight figure almost swamped in the crowd, proud as a peacock. At eighty she still had pride in her looks. She was a beautiful, delicate china doll, much prettier than I could ever be, with porcelain features, a beautiful skin and a mass of fine white hair.

Everyone was in love with her and, in her eighties, she still had spirit enough to find flirting fun. She had great wit and humour, too. When her sister, my Aunt Kit, visited us from Canada, the two of them would keep each other in stitches swapping saucy jokes. The sight of those dear old white-haired ladies telling each other little-girl dirty jokes used to break me up.

There was one occasion when all the disappointment, all the struggling to reach some sort of recognition became worth while for me; distilled into the look on my mother's face as she sat by my side in her best coat and hat on a specially constructed platform in the middle of

Manchester's Piccadilly. It was Christmas time and I had been asked to switch on the lights of the city. I coaxed mum to come along. They sent a Rolls Royce to fetch us. The square was swamped with people and police had to clear a path for us through the crowd. I pulled the switch that lit up Manchester, the band played, the crowds cheered and surged forward and my mother, bursting with pride, waved a regal acknowledgement from her seat of honour. Autograph books and pieces of paper were thrust at her. She signed them all "Elsie Tanner's Mother". Bless her. Without her and Tony Warren, Elsie T. would have never existed.

For a while I lived in a cottage in the small country village of Hayfield, near Manchester.

Tony Warren lived in the cottage opposite us. He and I used to go for long muddy walks on winter afternoons wrapped in mufflers and wearing Wellingtons. We had just started in the *Street* and, without tuppence for the taxi, he would meet me at the railway station and we would walk over wet fields home, him in my sou'wester which he took a fancy to. The locals found Tony rather exotic, but then he is not exactly formal in his behaviour. At our first visit to the yokel-filled village pub he astonished everyone by stretching his six-foot-three flat out on the floor quoting the service of exorcism in sonorous tones. We had been discussing spiritualism and exorcism in general when Tony was reminded of something he he had once seen and, being Tony, he thought nothing of demonstrating it. It caused quite a stir but I honestly don't think he noticed. The pub is called the Lantern Pike and Tony says he took the landlady as the model for Annie Walker.

"But the *nice* part of Annie Walker," he hastens to add.

Tony is, without a doubt, the wittiest, funniest person I know. But even when he is being perfectly serious, the effect of his "outré" behaviour on solid citizens can send me hysterical.

Tony triggers off extraordinary events simply by being Tony. Once at Granada he was telling somebody that in spite of being six-foot-three, he was slim enough to fit into the drawer of a filing cabinet. They were sceptical. Being Tony he set out to prove it. He folded himself into the drawer and bade the other fellow shut it. He did. Just then, one of Granada's top bosses walked into the office. Tony remained rigid, folded into the drawer for ten minutes until he left. All he said when finally released was: "There! I told you I could."

Tony, for all the laughter, wit and humour, is a very sensitive person with an enormous talent. Inside there is a sensitive clock ticking away. His humour is never cruel, his wit never debases. He is a good and loyal friend and I love him. We look back often to those Hayfield days.

My mother had continued to live in the council house in Rosedale Road, Manchester, where we had lived for years. Her health was not good and I decided she must come and live near me. I found a derelict Georgian house in Sale, Cheshire. I called it "Derrygill" after my mother's farm in Ireland. All the Georgian character had been knocked out of it over the years so Bill and I set about restoring it. There was nothing much left but the skirting boards. It had an acre of ground which was like a jungle. I shall never forget the night Bill and Arthur Lowe went round the grounds carrying two glasses and a Jeroboam of Champagne, fighting their way through ten-feet-tall sticks of rhubarb, deciding where to put the rose beds and the swimming pool. I could not conceive it then, but in no time at all we had three thousand roses and a heated swimming pool just where they had said they would be. It was not a big house; four rooms upstairs and four rooms down. We moved mother to a house in the next street. She would not move into Derrygill for fear of losing her independence. For six years I lived there and eventually moved on the advice of my doctor, who said it was too near the river and the chemical works. The rising mists from the Mersey were doing nasty things to my lungs.

We found and fell in love with a sixteen-roomed mansion at Disley in Yorkshire. It had, apart from the sixteen rooms, just for the hell of it, a full-sized billiard room. Mother agreed to move with us, just as long as she could have her own apartment. The house was certainly big enough and a separate annexe was earmarked and converted for her use. She had her own kitchen, bathroom, sitting room and bedroom and bought all her own food. I don't know why she bothered because she was in with us all day and ate all her meals in our dining room. But she clung tenaciously to the idea of her independence and we all kept up the pretence that she did not really live with us at all.

"I have my own place, you know," she would explain carefully to visitors.

Tony Warren and my mother were great friends. Each appreciated the other's humour and they adored each other for it. Tony always claims that when my mother first set eyes on Parkhill, as the Disley mansion was called, she refused to be impressed. Standing in the hall, gazing up at the curving staircase and vaulted ceiling, she said (according to Tony's version): "Ah, but I was used to *really* high ceilings in Rosedale Road." (Rosedale Road was a Council house!)

Mother claimed she never said that at all, but simply: "It was cosier in Rosedale Road."

Parkhill was always full of people and parties. We would leave the door open all the time and everybody came to stay.

It was fun to play lady of the manor at Disley and give

elegant dinner parties for a dozen or more people. I was never allowed to play the part to the full, however. At least, not when Doreen Murphy had anything to do with it. Doreen I have known since both of us were little girls. My mother was always "Aunt Nan" to Doreen. Doreen's mum, Dolly, and mine had been great friends in their youth. From time to time at Disley she consented to come and housekeep for me, which she did in her own inimitable manner.

There I would sit at one end of the large oval dining table, gowned and bejewelled, candles glowing, appreciative dinner guests to my right and left. Picking up a small bell I would ring prettily for Doreen to bring in the next course. Tinkle . . . tinkle . . .

No reaction.

Tinkle, tinkle (a bit firmer this time). Then from the kitchen would come Doreen's tall spare figure, two curlers inadvertently left in the front of her hair, a sort of defiant substitute for a lace cap.

"What's up wi' you, flower," she would demand in blunt Lancashire. "I've only one pair of 'ands, you know."

My mother enjoyed all the hustle and bustle and comings and goings. Once, at a New Year's Eve party, I found her sitting on the stairs with two of the local constabulary who had wandered in to wish us a Happy New Year. She did not take at all kindly to the idea of a life of retirement. Once I found a beautiful remote farmhouse, set in thirty acres of moorland. The nearest dwelling was a pub, a mile down the road. I was keen to buy it and I took mother to see it. She didn't fancy the idea at all. As we drove along, leaving habitation further and further behind, she got quieter and quieter. Spry as a two-year-old when we left Disley, she seemed to become older and older as the miles increased.

When we got to the front of the farmhouse she resembled Rider Haggard's "She" – after, not before! She reached for a stick she hadn't used for months and hobbled painfully up to the door. Bent over, she tottered through the door, glanced fearfully at the winding staircase and practically crawled up it on her hands and knees.

"Oh, I'll never manage these stairs," she sighed to herself, for my benefit. "What if I get ill? Who'll come and see me all the way out here?" What an actress! Mother had made up her mind. She had no intention of moving.

All the way home she was chirpy as a chicken, shedding a year for each mile that took the farmhouse further away. She had made her point. I admitted defeat. Mother was great with the horses. She could always pick a winner and enjoyed betting, even though she thought it was sinful. When I went out in the morning I would give her a fiver and tell her to put it on a horse.

"Did it win?" I would ask her later.

"Oh, yes," she'd say.

"Then you've got a lot of money."

"Well, I only put a bob each way on it."

Somehow it seemed less of a sin to her if she only put a shilling on instead of a fiver.

She was a great judge of character in some ways, but was really mistaken in her opinion of some actresses. She was convinced that the theatrical profession was full of whores. Everyone who came to the house got a quick once over and woe betide them if they didn't measure up. Mother wasn't one to hide her feelings. We would often have the most terrible rows and stand there screaming at each other. Bill always used to say we were both saying exactly the same thing but not listening to each other. He was right, too. I was certainly no "little Miss Precious Boots" to her. Hell on wheels was more like it. I felt the back of her hand more than once. When I was forty she slapped me across the face at a party for using a four-letter word. And she did it in full view of producers, writers, directors — the entire showbiz world.

"Don't ever let me hear you use that word again," she said. To my credit, I seldom do.

To her I was always a child. Three weeks before she died she said to me: "I'm feeling very tired. I should like to go to sleep."

I pretended I did not know what she was talking about. Her spirit was sinking, her heart was failing, she was living on borrowed time. I was aware of all this, but she was preparing me. Each day for her was becoming more and more of an agony.

"Go to sleep then, if you're tired," I said, blinking hard to hold back the tears and pretending that she meant an ordinary night's sleep.

"If I go to sleep," she said, "what are you going to do?"

Very roughly, because I couldn't bear it, I said: "Oh, I'm a big girl now."

"You'll never be a big girl," she said. "Not as long as you live."

I believe she was staying alive for me. Three weeks later she died.

Chapter Thirty-Three

The Disley house was far enough away from Manchester to make travelling in to the studios every day a chore, especially in foggy weather. I don't drive and Bill had to pick me up or I had to take a taxi. So I rented a flat in Manchester and stayed there when I was working late at the studios and on transmission days.

Mother was fine when I left Disley in the morning; up and about, spry and cheerful. The next morning Margot Bryant asked me how she was and instead of saying, "She's fine" I said: "I don't know, Margot. I have an odd feeling."

The feeling was so strong that I telephoned home and they told me she was sleeping. It was transmission day and we were very busy but I could not shake off the feeling of foreboding; the feeling that something was amiss. That evening after the show Bill and Harry Kershaw walked into my dressing room. Bill looked at me and put his hand on my shoulder.

"Don't go any further," I said. "I know. She's dead."

She had been dead when I called home but they did not want to tell me until the show was finished. Harry and Bill just stood looking at me. I could not cry. I just pushed past them out of the room.

"Let me out," I said. "I have to take a walk."

I walked round and round and round the corridors of Granada. I don't know for how long. I had a terrible unreasoning anger against people who lived on while she was dead. I was angry with the life she had had; I was angry with me for being what I was to her when I should have been so much more; I was angry for all the times I had been such a bitch; angry for all the times I had left her on her own. I kept that anger up for three months; it was my only defence against the loss of her.

I never set much store by my relatives. Except for my cousin Ivy and Aunt Kit, I never gave a snap for any of them. And no less so than on the day of my mother's funeral. I remember years back in childhood during the Depression my mother trying to borrow some small amount of money from relatives who owned a shop. The money was to help my stepfather out of debt. They could not find it in their hearts or their purses to lend her two pence. She went to the pawn shop instead and with what cost to her pride. I have even less time for the relatives who, when I became successful, were suddenly anxious to claim kinship. Some of them turned out in force for the funeral. I stood at the top of the stairs and watched them. My own pain was so intense I could only hold myself together with anger. I watched two young cousins who had been genuinely fond of my mother getting rather tearful.

"You can stop that before you start," I said through tight lips. "Don't let me see you weeping." And I added, rather unfairly, "You couldn't care less about her while she lived. Why waste your tears now."

Somebody came up and put a hand on my arm.

"Auntie Pat . . ."

I rounded on them.

"Don't you 'Auntie Pat' me."

I can imagine the thoughts of the casual observers.

"Typical. Dry-eyed at her own mother's funeral. Well, she always was as hard as nails."

But I must not cry. If I cried I would melt away and any spirit, character and backbone – all the gifts she had given me – would run away into the gutter and down the drain. My only defence was in tight-lipped rage. I had to stay angry.

I believe now, as I did then, that any good qualities I have came from her. But I also believed without her I would crumble; my backbone would melt like wax. I used to think that when she went Pat Phoenix would disintegrate. She had given me strength during her life and I adored her so. She was strong in terrible sickness and adversity. I am only one-tenth the woman she was; just the comma that comes after the sentence.

Today, after a journey of any distance, my first impulse is to pick up a phone and let Mum know I have arrived safely. Or to dash out and buy a present to take home to her. And then I realise that she is no longer there.

I have never been tempted to "talk" to my mother; to try and contact her at a seance, although I am somewhat psychic. The only time I ever attended a seance *I* fell into a trance. It was in Keighley and someone suggested we go along for a laugh. We all sat there in the dark and the last thing I remember was feeling sleepy. When I awoke I was in a chair with six people round me. I had been talking in an old lady's voice, shouting: "I'm falling. I'm falling." When we got back to our digs we discovered that one of the old ladies who ran the place had fallen downstairs while we were out.

The second time it happened to me was in Merthyr

Tydfil. I became friendly with the town's Registrar and he took me to tea to meet his mother. It was a very old house where they lived with a lovely old-fashioned kitchen – Welsh dressers and willow pattern plates. His mother sat rocking in an old chair. The scene was picturesque but, as soon as I walked through the door, I felt something. An awful depression descended on me and I began to weep.

"Oh, look now," the old lady chuckled. "We'd better get her upstairs. She realises what has happened here."

I felt an awful fool but they seemed to take the whole thing for granted. They would not tell me what happened in the kitchen except to say that it was the most awful tragedy.

When something like that happens today, I simply say it is my antennae twitching. I seem to have an extra sense that picks up people's distress. Even when I don't know the person very well, I get a sense of real pain from them. I passed someone at Granada in the corridors once and a wave of emotion hit me. I grabbed his arm and said: "For God's sake. What ails you?"

He looked at me in amazement.

"How did you guess? I thought I was hiding it so well."

My mother was like that, too. I think it is the Irish in us. I could not explain to him but I had known he was suffering deeply. With my mother, I could be miles away but know instantly when she was ill. One weekend I travelled home from the far south of the country to see mother, when I could ill afford the fare, because I had the feeling she was sick. She was, but had forbidden anyone to write and tell me. There was, you might say, a very strong umbilical cord between us.

Of all the ways I failed her – and they were many – I gave her one thing. I had succeeded when all had prophesied failure. I had fulfilled my mother's dream – or at least part of it.

I see her now in Piccadilly, Manchester, turning on the lights. Duodenal ulcers, angina, frail and white-haired, but spirited as they come, sitting there dressed in her best and saying with great satisfaction: "Yes. I am Elsie Tanner's mother."

Chapter Thirty-Four

Elsie Tanner must fall in love again decreed the programme planners in 1970.

"Oh, no," I wailed. "I don't want another boy-friend.
Enough is enough."

It had long ago been decided not to force any of us to do
anything we felt was out of character, but this time producer
Harry Kershaw was adamant.

"You've got to have another boy-friend," he insisted.

"I'm not, I'm not," I protested madly. "I'm getting too
old for that sort of thing."

"You're never too old," laughed Harry. "I'll tell you
what," he cajoled. "We'll let you pick him."

Mollified, I narrowed the choice down to two. Jack
Elam, a marvellous actor, who plays the mean, menacing
villain in all those John Wayne Westerns, was my first but
Harry said he would look a bit out of place in Salford. Next
I chose another American, Peter Falk, now famous as
television's brilliant but short-sighted detective, Columbo.
Another superb actor to my mind. Harry looked up from
his manuscript-laden desk and said: "What *is* this obsession
with one-eyed actors? Anyway, we'd never get a work

permit for them and how do you think they would look standing next to Lucille buying twenty fags from the corner shop?"

He looked at me laughingly: "Try someone English," he said. "If you had your pick of English actors – money no object – who would you have?"

I had just been watching an actor do a beautiful Russian, Kamarov, in *Special Branch*. I looked at Harry for a moment, our minds must have been working on the same frequency.

"How about . . ." he said.

"Alan Browning," I finished.

It was, I promise, a purely professional decision on my part although I must confess it idly crossed my mind that he was an attractive man whenever I watched him on television. I had thought him outstandingly good in *Nana* and had loved his performance in *The War of Darkie Pillbeam* which Tony Warren wrote for Granada, and had even stopped him in the studio corridor to tell him how good I thought he was.

We would exchange brief "Good Mornings" as we passed after that when Alan was appearing in a Granada programme and he has since told me that he often paused to watch me "Swinging your hips down the corridor". Saucy devil.

But selecting him for my screen boy-friend was not a romantic affair. It was simply that I admired the man's acting tremendously. We were not sure if he would come. Harry felt he might not be keen to go into another long running series after his long spell in *The Newcomers*. But he agreed to an initial thirteen weeks on the show. Joan Gray, his agent, was a friend of mine from years back.

"If you and Pat Phoenix meet it will either be a head-on clash or the romance of the century," she told Alan. In the beginning it was neither. He came into the show and although I was rather nervous of working with someone I respected so much as an actor, I found him a nice man. No more. Just a nice man.

I used to have a regular girl's night out with Adele Rose, one of *Coronation Street*'s finest scriptwriters and a great friend. Our nights on the town were a riot. Once at the Playboy Club in London they got me to dress up as a bunny girl and I went around the cocktail bar serving drinks with a practised bunny dip. I got quite good at it and anyway, in that costume, I didn't dare bend over! We had ways of discouraging enthusiastic gentlemen who attempted to join our company. One was to get the head waiter to present them with our usually very large bill, the minute they sat themselves down uninvited at our table.

That "night" finished up in the early morning with bacon and eggs at the club's breakfast bar. Adele headed the queue and I was third in line. Adele held her hand out for a plate. Plate she didn't get – breakfast she did. The chef suddenly spotted me in the line. Staring fixedly at me he swiftly shovelled hot bacon and greasy eggs on to Adele's outstretched bare palm. Her face was a picture I shall never forget.

One of our evening's out ended at the house of a mutual friend where we met up with the crowd. Alan had been with the *Street* for some three weeks then and just in passing I happened to mention what a super gentleman he was. That was a mistake. The most my mates had heard me say about a fellow was "He's all right". Whooping with glee they literally dragged me off down to the pub where Alan was staying. Tommy Mann, stunt man for Granada, ushered me in. I remember Georgie Best was behind the bar that night and all the lads were there. There was a curious silence when I walked in because they knew that I do not frequent pubs, particularly late at night. Then Tommy announced in a voice of thunder: "Pat Phoenix to see Mr. Alan Browning."

I could have killed him. Poor Alan was not even there. He had decided on an early night and was in bed when the manager of the place rushed into his room and said: "Get up! She's here!"

"Who?" said Alan drowsily.

"Pat Phoenix," the manager told him.

Poor Alan had to drag himself out of bed and come downstairs, dragging on his shirt. I felt awful and was so embarrassed but fortunately he sensed it. Everybody was looking at us and I was stiff and formal.

"I'm terribly sorry," I told him, looking rather po-faced, "but this is nothing whatsoever to do with me."

Alan grinned delightedly.

"Maybe not," he said. "But I'm glad you came."

I thawed and we talked. He told me of his long separation from his wife of which I had not been aware and I, over eager to put the record straight, told him that I really didn't have much interest in romantic attachments. A week later we had a love scene in the script. He took me in his arms and kissed me and the director had to shout "cut!" four times before we heard him.

When it comes to love and romance I am a very slow moving lady but on this occasion the bomb went off right under me. As it says in the script, I was in it before I knew. It was Smithie, my Corgi, who showed me how much I was beginning to care for Alan. Poor Smithie got a bone stuck in his throat and was choking. Alan and I knelt down side by side on the rug while he gently pulled the bone from the dog's mouth. Our eyes met and on the commonplace, not very romantic occasion, we both knew something wonderful was happening.

With me it is a case of love me, love my dogs, and no matter how gone I was on him, no matter how much he attracted me, if he had not liked dogs he could have gone out that front door faster than anybody. Instead he came through the door – to stay. And then the rumours began to fly.

One night we came home together from a function and, contrary to general opinion about the life style of television stars, Alan was making tea in the kitchen in his stocking feet and I, with a tea towel round my waist, was buttering toast. The door bell rang.

"Who the hell is that," said Alan. "It's eleven o'clock."

It was the Press, with a camera and a foot in the door.

"What the hell . . ." I echoed.

"Before you start, Miss Phoenix," said one, throwing down the sort of challenge I was always unable to resist, "we have been watching you for several days. We have taken pictures of you with a telescopic lens and we have made inquiries of other people living in this building. Now, are you living together? Do you plan to marry? Is it just an affair?"

Vesuvius erupted! The words that poured from my lips were neither English, pretty nor printable. They threatened us with "intimate" photographs. It turned out later that they had taken pictures at a charity Press ball of Alan and I holding hands and dancing cheek to cheek. Intimate pictures! Anybody would have thought we had streaked through Piccadilly in the rush hour.

Alan is a more reasonable soul than I, thank God, and with fifteen years of journalism behind him he was able to cope with the situation far better than I. While I frothed, stormed, raged and stamped all over the carpet, screaming about the KGB, creepy crawlies and spies, he offered them both a gin and tonic. He pacified them by saying if there was a story to tell we would tell it tomorrow as it was getting late and we all needed our sleep. And besides it would take him half an hour to fasten Miss Phoenix into her strait-jacket after the fit they had brought on by their unannounced arrival.

They departed and we rang Norman Frisby, Granada's Press Officer, immediately.

"The best way to kill a story," he advised, "as you well know, Alan, is to give a 'no story'. In other words we'll call a conference tomorrow and tell 'em all."

The headlines next day told the story of our non-engagement and how we liked each other but that no one was thinking about marriage.

"It's always manners to wait until asked," I quoted at forty-two bulb flashing pressmen.

"How can I ask her," said Alan. "I am still married."

That was the story, front page, all editions, and in fact it said nothing. But somebody was thinking about marriage – not for Pat Phoenix and Alan Browning but for Elsie Tanner and Alan Howard.

Producer, June Howson, sympathising with my impatience at the long stream of boy-friends who were successively following Mrs. Tanner into middle-age, felt like me, it was time she married. And who more suitable than the charming Alan Howard. But even the path of our screen love was not to run smoothly. Controversy raged among the scriptwriters. Some said the pair should wed and some said they should not.

Chapter Thirty-Five

There was some skirmishing on the side between unrelated scriptwriters Adele and Esther Rose, when Esther maintained that a man like Alan Howard would not marry a woman like Elsie Tanner.

"She's much too common for him," claimed Esther.

"What!" cried Adele, outraged. And enunciating very clearly she declared: "Elsie Tanner is all things to all men. She is *just* the sort of woman that Alan Howard would fall for."

The "ayes" won the day and Elsie Tanner became Mrs. Howard in a July wedding. In contrast to the previous wedding to Steve Tanner, this time we were married at a quiet little Registrar's Office in Wilmslow, Cheshire. The first thought was to marry us in a pretty little Wilmslow church until they realised we had both in the script been married before. It was most romantically filmed by one-time director and cameraman Eric Prytherch who was later to become the producer of *Coronation Street*. I chose a grey suit and matching hat. Julie Goodyear was bridesmaid and the best man was — who but Peter Adamson. The public set their seal of approval on this latest wedding with cards, flowers and presents.

I found that when I made personal appearances alone the public would not only ask "How's Len?" but "Where's your dishy husband?" I think quietly the public would have liked me to be married to both of them at the same time. The viewers took to Alan in a big way and we began to get letters addressed to "Mr. and Mrs. Howard". One from the matron of an old ladies' home told us that one of the inmates was very poorly and would be enormously cheered by a letter from Alan and me. It was near Christmas and it was just as easy for us to send a hamper as it was to send a card.

Alan Browning, who is very much a man's man, chose every single article that went into that hamper. He did not, as some might do, get someone else to do it for him. Pondering as each article went into the basket, "Now do you think that's suitable for an old lady?" and "Do you think they would like that?" Thank God nobody is ever daft enough to ask me why I love him. They wrote back with a photograph they had taken of their room and it was covered from floor to ceiling with pictures of Alan and me.

Not long after our "wedding" we heard from a woman who told us her mother, who was eighty-odd, had no television set but loved *Coronation Street*. The old lady liked to go round to her daughter's house to watch it but when her daughter was out she would go round to a television shop window where a set was on at night and, standing in the street, would watch through the window. Now she was ill at her home and she missed *Coronation Street* and would very much appreciate a letter from us. I began to reply but then I noticed the address was not far from the studio.

Alan was away and on impulse as usual, I said to Bill,

who was busily managing all my affairs: "It's daft sending her this note. Come on. Let's go round."

So Bill went out and bought some flowers and fruit and over we went to Salford. We stopped in a street not unlike Coronation Street and knocked on the door of a little two up and two down. The daughter opened it and she just stood and stared in astonishment.

From the front room we heard a quavering voice: "Who is it then, luv? Is it insurance come?"

"No, mum," said the daughter in a dazed voice. "It's Elsie Tanner and a fella."

We went into the lounge where she lay on a sofa bed. She knew me instantly and was suddenly spry as a chicken and shouting to her daughter: "Make 'em a cup of tea."

Then to us: "Move that paper. Sit down! Sit down! Ee, where's me teeth."

It was a short visit, prolonged only by Bill asking for a second cup of tea. We kissed her goodbye and she, a bit choked up, thanked us for coming to see her. I wanted to say, "Thank *you* for standing outside in the cold to watch us through a shop window."

But it seemed a bit sloppy.

Chapter Thirty-Six

Something very odd was going on in our house. Alan was getting mysterious telephone calls and whenever I came into the room he hung up. Once I heard him say: "I can't talk now. She's coming in."

Now I'm not jealous by nature but I was beginning to get a bit suspicious – but then my birthday was coming up – and knowing Alan, he could be planning a surprise. He was going out more frequently, too. When I asked him where he was going he would say airily: "Just popping over to Stockport to see my mother."

Now, Alan is very fond of his mother and visits her often – but four times in one week!

Alan and Elsie Howard were supposed to be having a big night out in the script. It entailed night shooting on the outside set of the *Street*.

"Wear one of your own dresses for the scene," said producer, Eric Prytherch.

"Thank you very much," I retorted indignantly. Was he suggesting you couldn't tell the difference between our evening gowns and the dresses more suited to Elsie?

"Well, it's a very special occasion for her," he hedged.

"Alan is taking her out and she would have spent a lot of money."

"Elsie Tanner would not spend that amount on an evening dress. She could not afford it, you Welsh nitwit," I scolded.

I couldn't figure it out. Here he was urging me to wear something fancy when usually he was complaining I spent too much. He made such a fuss about what I wore, too.

"Something with a bit of cleavage, you know," he kept suggesting.

It was winter and I had a cold. I wasn't too keen on hanging around outside in an evening dress freezing to death; in fact I was playing hell about it.

"You're trying to kill me off, aren't you?" I complained.

"You can put your mink coat round your shoulders," said Taff.

"What!" I cried. "For the take! You must be out of your mind. A posh dress is one thing, but you can't put Elsie in a mink."

Taff looked confused.

"Oh, I was forgetting," he said lamely.

Peter, Alan and I were just getting ready for the take – I was moaning bitterly about the cold and couldn't understand why Peter and Alan kept grinning – when I heard those four little words that must have struck a chill into most who hear them.

"Patricia Phoenix. This is your life."

And there was Eamonn Andrews.

It seems that friend Keith McDonald, a journalist on the *Manchester Evening News*, overhearing a conversation in a television studio about the next *This Is Your Life* subject, suggested Pat Phoenix.

"We can't get her," they said. "She is working in Manchester." Keith suggested they do it live and the whole of Granada television co-operated. That is how Eamonn Andrews came to be wandering down Coronation Street with a red book in his hand with my name on the cover. When I realised what was happening, I panicked.

"Taff, I'll bloody kill you," I said to our luckless producer. They had all been involved in the plot. I think everyone's first instinct must be to run away. I know I was frightened to death.

I backed away trying to escape through a door of anonymity but Peter, Alan and Eamonn held on like grim death.

My confrontation with Eamonn had to go out live. Apart from the fact that I rarely visit London, Alan and I were sitting watching *This Is Your Life* one night when the subject had been conned into going to a dinner at a television centre. I said to Alan: "Nobody would ever catch me with one of those lunches or dinners."

So they rigged it on the set instead.

After meeting Eamonn and composing myself, they took me to a hotel in Manchester where the rest of the programme was filmed. All I could think of was that whoever came on the floor I must instantly recognise them whether I really did or not. I need not have been so anxious. I knew them all at once. As anyone who has been on *This Is Your Life* knows, it is a very genuinely emotional thing. My brain was going thud, thud, thud with the effort to think who would come on next and I was so busy worrying about them that I didn't have time to worry about myself.

All my mates from *Coronation Street* were there. It *had* struck me when I came into the studio earlier that the cast were all dressed up like dog's dinners for some reason. It even occurred to me they might be snubbing me and had all arranged to go somewhere without me.

The day before I was moaning to Doris about my

dreadful cold and having to do an outside shot feeling the way I did.

"Well, I'm just not going to turn up," I told her. She rushed off to Alan in a panic.

"Alan, Alan, Pat says she's not turning up tomorrow."

"Now, you know what she's like," soothed Alan. "Pat's just blowing off. She'll be there."

And I was. So were many dear faces from my years in rep, like lovely Charles Simon and Marilyn Thomas. Sandy Powell, with whom I made *Cup Tie Honeymoon* all those years ago, came along and one of my best-loved teachers from central school days and many, many other dear and familiar faces. And, most important of all, my beloved Aunt Kit flew in from Canada.

When it was all over I suddenly thought of something extraordinary. That my best friends, all of whom I thought I knew so well, had turned out without exception to be the most accomplished and practised liars. And so had Alan! Visiting his mother, indeed.

We had a steaming row about it.

"My God!" I raged at him. "You've got a marvellous talent for lying."

"Ah, well," I heard him tell a friend later, "I told you what she'd say when they said 'Patricia Phoenix. This is your life.' She'll say, 'Alan Browning. This is my fist.' "

Chapter Thirty-Seven

People were obviously happy to see Alan and I together but
the big question between us was should we turn our screen
marriage into a real marriage. I am a Sagittarian and,
according to the stars, if you believe in that sort of thing,
those born under that particular sign are constantly on the
run from the marriage bed and all that goes with it. Having
had one disastrous marriage this was doubly true for me. I
was scared and I don't care who knows it. Not that Alan
hadn't all the qualifications of a super husband but that I
had none of a good wife.

But miraculously, with all my myriad faults, he loved me.
I couldn't understand it. I can't to this day. I loved him,
too, but the battle for and against marriage was on. I told
him we could go on together for ever and ever but no
marriage. I did not want it.

"It spoils things for people," I said. I could hear my
father's voice: "If I can't have my child at least give me my
record."

And my mother's echoing: "Don't ever get married.
It's not worth the unhappiness."

I was determined I was never going to do it again. I

knew that I was too wrapped up in the job I was doing. I was totally selfish of my creature comforts. Things like reading 'til three in the morning, making tea at five, leaving the top off the toothpaste, scratch meals. What man would put up with that? A man has to be ten feet tall to witness head waiters presenting his wife with the bill and having people refer to her as a single entity throughout their wedded life. But here was such a man. Strong enough in his own career not to be intimidated by the gay caparisons of mine. Suddenly I felt I was being even more selfish by not marrying him. Here was a man who needed the partner of his choice. He wanted it right or not at all. It finished up with me proposing to him. We set the date for Christmas Eve, 1972. My excuse for that was that people would not have to buy us two presents.

My friends were delighted; others said, "Poor sod. Fancy being married to a bitch like that."

I secretly agreed with them.

There were even those who told me I was an idiot and that I did not need marriage. There were the doom prophets, the head shakers and the finger waggers, but not dear Peter Adamson who was simply delighted for me as were Bill, Graham, Diana and all my other friends. Lovely Doris Speed gagged to Alan: "You're making a dreadful mistake, you know. I'm the wealthy one, not her."

Violet, who adores Alan, was touchingly concerned for me.

"Now, Pat, are you sure you are doing the right thing," she asked. "You know what you are when you lose your freedom. You get all fidgety."

I was very nervous and apprehensive. These things are usually attributed to the groom. Doris wagged a finger at me and said: "Don't start regretting your freedom before you've lost it."

She and Alan share a running gag. It is meant for my eyes only. She insists on hitching up her stockings in front of him, not much further than the knee I might add, and flashing him a cod, coy look. He declares she is driving him wild with temptation. I tell her I am madly jealous and I know perfectly well that she and Alan have been having an affair for years. She dissolves into laughter. Her sense of humour is the best I've yet come across. She is witty, camp and Coward-ish and we both adore her. Her wedding present was as sparkling as she herself – an enormous crate of champagne.

Chapter Thirty-Eight

A small wedding, I said.

About eight people, I said.

No more, I said.

You're dead right, agreed Alan.

We felt we could not have everybody from *Coronation Street* so we would have just a couple of our closest friends from the cast. It was decided; a small wedding. Or so I thought.

Alan had been sitting with his mate, Bernard Youens, and Jean Alexander, who play Stan and Hilda Ogden. Bernard was to be an usher at the wedding and as they made plans Alan turned to Jean and said: "You're coming, aren't you?"

She must have been surprised into saying "Yes" because Jean and I simply did not hit it off. This is not her fault but mine. We are poles apart. She is a quiet, reserved person and I, in my big, noisy, overflowing way, am an irritant to her. Alan was as aware of this as anybody but in his big-mouthed, out-going way he had asked her and he was not going back on the invitation.

When he told me I hit the roof.

"I thought it was going to be a small wedding," I blazed. "You start that and you have to ask everybody."

But Alan was firm.

"I'm not going back on the invitation," he told me. "Bunny and Jean go together and they are both friends of mine. I meant the invitation, and it is my wedding, too, you know."

That night we were driving past a little Catholic church and I called Alan to stop. I feel sometimes in need of soul food and I find it in this quiet little church, called the "hidden gem" because of its anonymity, crammed as it is between offices and factories in a backwater of the city. When the Father sees me there he gives me a little wink and a smile. Once he caught me bringing flowers and thanked me.

"Don't thank me," I called, retreating out of the door. "I'm not a Catholic."

"I know, I know," he reassured me in his soft, Irish brogue. "But come in just the same."

That night I sat until all the wrath and bitching boiled out of me. Then I went back to Alan where he waited in the car and told him I had made up my mind. I was going to invite everybody to the wedding.

When everybody was coming Jean decided she wasn't. Since I always thought her feelings for me were something like other people feel for cockroaches I was not at heart surprised. But I knew what I must do. I went to her and said: "Please come, Jean, for my sake. I want you there." And I meant it.

She softened at that and, for a minute, I think we reached out and touched each other. East is still east and west is still west but I will never forget that when I asked her for something, she gave. She came to my wedding and what is more had a ball. It was a super present she gave; a silver butler's tray. When I see it shining on my old oak sideboard I am reminded never to judge things too hastily.

We still live in different worlds, still see things differently, but I think we have been a bit closer since that day. However opposed our opinions may be, Jean Alexander is a reserved, sensitive, honest person and I am a big loud mouth. So take that, Miss Phoenix.

Chapter Thirty-Nine

It's a funny thing to say about a wedding but mine was murder. For a start I was suffering from severe congestion of the lungs, I was booked for a couple of heavy public appearances the week before and, as if that were not enough, Elsie and Alan Howard were having one of their big moments in the *Street*.

I was coming home exhausted from the studio and throwing myself into the wedding arrangements. Unlike most brides I had no fond mum and dad to make sure every thing went off all right. Alan and I had to stage-manage the whole affair ourselves.

First we had to find a church willing to marry us; both Alan and I being divorced. We wanted a church wedding ourselves and felt that other people wanted it for us, too. The Reverend William Riley promised to conduct the service in the grey and blue Etherow Brow Methodist Chapel in the village of Broadbottom, a ten-minute drive from my home.

I designed the costumes; Alan stage-managed. My beautiful cake was baked by an old childhood friend who lived next door to me in schooldays – Ada Moulson. My wedding

outfit was a purple velvet cape over layers of white petticoats. The cape was trimmed with white kolinsky fox
fur and I carried a matching muff, holly and mistletoe
trimmed – the magic bough. No dressmaker could get the
idea of what I wanted so, in the end, I went to a theatrical
costumier. I had four matrons of honour. One was Irene
Sutcliffe, who was, of course, Maggie Clegg of the corner
shop before she left in June, 1974. The others were
Coronation Street scriptwriter Adele Rose, my cousin, Ivy,
and Bill Nadin's wife, Linda. They all looked beautiful in
full length lavender wool skirts, deep purple blouses and
short lavender capes. I had a touching letter from a little
eight-year-old girl called Maxine Ferrell, who wrote and
asked if she could be bridesmaid. I had to write and tell her
that I had chosen my bridesmaids and they were all ladies.
But she came along as a sort of "special bridesmaid". I told
her what colour I would be wearing and, looking pretty
as a picture, she matched me in a dress of royal blue velvet.
We had our own "special" wedding picture taken together
and it is in my album.

I awoke the morning of the wedding feeling half dead
and with five ridges across my cheek where Alan had belted
me the day before. On purpose, too – just as we had
planned it. He had to hit me in the script and I had to
wallop him back. We decided an unconvincing tap was no
good. It had to be a real good thump. I braced myself and
he really let me have it. The trouble was I mark easily and
it took several layers of make-up to disguise the clout from
the congregation, the crowds outside, not to mention the
officiating minister.

My dress weighed a ton and my bridesmaids were so
busy getting themselves ready that I was helped into it by a
fella! Dear Harry Shelton, a good and kind friend for many
years, got me to the church on time, chivvying: "Come on,

luv, get your drawers on", as he snapped poppers and found my shoes.

As it happened, I arrived in my Rolls two minutes early to face a crowd of hundreds who had waited in the freezing cold to see me. Alan, immaculately handsome in a grey topper and tails and purple velvet cravat to match my dress, had arrived ten minutes earlier. He, his best man, Bill Nadin, ushers, Bernard Youens of the *Street* and a golfing mate Gerry Riley, whiled away the time making *sotto voce* jokes about my non-arrival. It was Lita Donne, Granada's young P.R.O. girl, whose protecting arm sheltered me from the pressing crowd.

For luck, I carried the gold ring I wore when I became Alan's TV wife in episode 1,002 of *Coronation Street*. If Alan had forgotten the real ring I was prepared! But he hadn't.

This time the wedding was for real. The theme was Christmas. The hymns were carols and the church was decorated with holly and mistletoe. Guests and sightseers jostled each other in the pews. The *Street* turned out in force "to see it done proper" – bless 'em. I came down the aisle on the arm of H.V.K. who was generously giving me away. The guests carolled forth with "God Rest Ye Merry, Gentlemen" in full voice – with the exception of the bride, who always sings off-key. The ceremony was simple – a new style service especially written for the Methodist Church. I had done what I said I never would do again.

Soon we were out in the biting winter air where a cheering crowd watched us drive off in an open vintage Rolls. It might have looked romantic but I was freezing to death. We held a reception for eighty guests in a pretty little hall in the middle of Hyde Park, far away from the crowds, the noise and the traffic. I get strange looks when I tell people I got married near Manchester and I held my reception in Hyde Park, but this one is in Cheshire. If I say so myself, the whole affair was well stage-managed and Alan and I did it all – props, wardrobe, lighting, cast, the lot!

That night we opened a bingo hall which we contracted to do before deciding the wedding date. When we got home I was on the point of exhaustion. Alan helped me out of my weighty wedding gown and I collapsed in his arms in a most un-bridelike way. I had severe congestion of the lungs and spent the whole of our so-called honeymoon period half unconscious – with two doctors in attendance – and Alan doing all the Christmas chores. Poor lad! What a way to start a marriage.

Chapter Forty

For me October 5th, 1973, was the day I burned the bridge that cut off Elsie Tanner's retreat. It was a bonfire that blazed all over the English (theatrical) countryside. For thirteen years she had loved, lost, laughed and lamented across millions of television screens twice a week, give or take a break or two. Time had wrought changes. She was no longer the blousy, buxom sex bomb of the early sixties, satin blouses slashed at the neck, beads and tight black skirts. With posh Alan Howard for a husband and a stainless steel sink unit installed at Number Eleven, Coronation Street, Elsie had reached respectability. It was time for me to say "tara" to Mrs. Tanner.

It was no sudden decision, I had been restless for some three years. Bryan Drew, my personal manager, in whose sound judgement I have complete trust, urged me often to make the break. The love of my husband, Alan, and his faith in me as an actress, strengthened my resolve.

It takes a certain kind of madness to give up the security of a steady job in a business not exactly noted for its pension rights. But security is not what being an actress is all about. Even so, me and Mrs. Tanner might have marched on for another couple of years but for Mr. Edward Heath and his pay freeze.

My contract ran out in May. I had not had a pay rise for three years but with the Freeze in force I accepted an interim six-month contract. In October negotiations began again. I was earning a substantial salary, but the cost of living was hitting me hard. We all had to keep up a certain standard – but, with the pay freeze, some of us were not just slipping a bit, we were sliding. After expenses I was left with very little. I have never been a worshipper at the feet of the Golden Ass, but I am an old fashioned believer that if you gain some sort of success, or whatever you like to call it, you owe the public something. They want a performance wherever you are. They want to see the circus with all the lights blazing and the calliope going full blast. They want to see the limousines, the furs, the jewellery and the make-up on your face must always be as perfect as you can make them, even if you are feeling like death. Someone at Granada once said to me that *Coronation Street* had made me a legend. It has been said often too that the ladies of *Coronation Street* are national monuments. The pigeons got at me a bit. I am no legend, neither then nor now, but for the sake of argument I said: "*If* I am a legend, the public did it and I invested money in that legend."

When Tony Warren used to call me "Catherine of all the bleeding Russias" and "The last of the Sunset Boulevards" (which he did with great affection) I would laugh but tell him: "All right. Say all those things. And keep saying them out loud."

Let's keep a bit of bezazz in the business. I have been told there were no "stars" in *Coronation Street*. I felt this oft repeated line was more than belittling after the years of hard work put in by the actors. If it gave us a lot, *we* also gave to it – blood. "We're *all* stars in *Coronation Street*," I was heard to mutter darkly, "every single one of us. If we weren't they could go out and take a picture of the bloody cobbles."

I am still nostalgically and lovingly connected with the *Street*. It's a family feeling. I think we all feel a bit that way. We can tell it off and bash it, but let someone else do it and we're in there fighting.

Bryan, my agent, warned me Granada felt they could not improve their offer and asked me if I was prepared to go all out – to do, as it were, or die. I told him "Yes". It was really much more than money that prompted me. Four years back I would have stayed in the *Street* no matter what others had offered in financial rewards. But the moving finger writes and having writ etc., Bryan released the announcement to the Press.

After thirteen years Miss Phoenix was on the wing. Phoenix flying free!

The truth was I was bored. Bored out of my mind. Going to the studios every day, hour after hour of waiting around to say four lines, getting home at the end of the day exhausted. Not because I was working hard, but because I wasn't. And worse than that I began to lose the ability to criticise my own performance. People would say, "You were marvellous last night."

Was I? I no longer knew if I was good, bad or indifferent. I was finally, after thirteen years, too close up, losing contact with the people who I was acting about and for. I had to get back in the mainstream again.

The break came easily. I had been released for thirteen weeks to tour in a stage play *Subway in the Sky*. In the script I had gone to Newcastle, a temporary ruse to cover my absence and one which the writers were able to make permanent by dint of Elsie's firm offering her a job there.

After three years in the *Street* Alan was restless, too.

Even if I had stayed on, I doubt he would. Quitting a series was no new experience for him. He left *The Newcomers* after two and a half years and was more used than me to the temperature of the water outside. Actor John Collins sent us a lovely, cheery telegram when the news was announced.

"Congratulations," it said. "It's a wonderful sunny morning. Come outside."

The twice weekly television appearance of Elsie Tanner had given me little opportunity to play other parts. I must have turned down some seventeen film roles because the schedules were too long. One I most regretted was a part in *Tom Jones*, which starred Albert Finney and Susannah York. I was offered a part in *Spring and Port Wine* but once again I was unable to accept. I declined with less regret than I might have. It was another North Country part, and to my mind I already had the best North Country part ever written.

In 1964 I did manage to squeeze a cameo part in *The L-Shaped Room* with Leslie Caron, in between appearing in *Coronation Street*, but only because they promised to complete shooting my role in four days. I played a cockney tart with a blonde wig which made a change from Elsie, if nothing else. Many of us on the *Street* felt the need of a rest from the routine of one character and one way of doing it was to go on tour in a stage play.

Granada released me to do a Tennessee Williams' play, *Suddenly Last Summer*. I played Catherine, a difficult, demanding and enormously satisfying role. The late Harry Driver, who wrote many *Coronation Street* scripts, saw me in Oldham. He came backstage afterwards virtually in a state of shock.

"You were marvellous," he said. "You frightened me to death. Why did you choose such a harrowing play?"

I was flattered and angry with him all at the same time. Flattered for his praise of my performance and angry that it had surprised him. The penance of playing one role for so long is that people think you are incapable of other portrayals. It might be true, but one hates to hear it!

My next stage venture was in 1970 when I played Annie Sullivan in *The Miracle Worker*. The role of the Irish woman who taught the youthful Helen Keller to communicate, was a role I had always wanted to do and it was made possible for me by Reg Marsh, who played bookie Dave Smith in the *Street*, and Bill Kenwright who played Gordon Clegg. Together they formed a company called David Gordon Productions and put the play on themselves. The tour was arranged so that most of the time I was within commuting distance of Granada Studios. It was hard work from the word go, but I thoroughly enjoyed it and it was a great success. It was also produced by friend and Director from Granada, Joe Boyer.

Working away from the *Street* as I was in *Subway in the Sky* when my decision to leave was made, I was spared the possibly traumatic moment of saying my last lines as Elsie Tanner. I had unknowingly said them some weeks previously.

I have been touched many times by the public's allegiance to Elsie Tanner but never more so than at the time of her departure from the *Street*. Letters poured in begging her to stay and, inevitably, many of the writers wished her well in her new life in Newcastle. But to my delight, Pat Phoenix got just as many letters from viewers hoping they would see *her* on television again soon.

After thirteen years of living with Elsie Tanner as my alter-ego, it was nice to know, that fond of her as I am, I was also wanted for myself.

One letter from a nine-year-old boy was very sweet. He

said he had cried when he heard I was leaving and that he hoped to marry me when he grew up. Reports of my age in newspaper stories of my departure had come as something of a surprise to him judging by the footnote to his letter. He wrote: "P.S. I thought you were twenty-five."

God bless him!

I don't suppose the public will ever let me forget Elsie, even if I wanted to, which I do not. Just after the news was out, I was rehearsing *Subway in the Sky* which was directed by William Franklyn, whose face is known to millions as the Schweppes man.

We were crossing the road together arm in arm after rehearsal one day when two lorry drivers, leaning against their wagons, spotted Bill. One shouted, in an incredulous voice, to his mate.

" 'Ere, look, Fred. It's 'im."

Small pause followed by startled double take.

"Bleedin' 'ell. 'e's with '*er*!"

We smiled into their disbelieving faces. I suppose Elsie Tanner and Mr. Schweppes did make an unlikely pair.

We rehearsed in London and, once again, the city's taxi drivers endeared themselves to my heart. There was one who took me back to my hotel and would not take the fare.

"My missus would kill me if I took money off of you," he said.

Once I stood in the pouring rain, dejected and nearly in tears from frustration for fifteen minutes trying to get a cab, when one with its "For Hire" sign unlit skidded to a stop.

" 'Op in," said the driver. "I'd 'ave only stopped fer you. I'm goine 'ome for me tea. Now, what's all this about you walking out on us . . ."

They are a smashing lot.

I won't pretend that leaving my mates on the *Street* wasn't something of a wrench. I miss them all, although we keep in close touch. They were wonderful years and I was privileged to work with a wonderful bunch of people. The *Street* was, and is, a success because of its people; actors, writers, producers, etc. All who have cared and still do. It is not a row of houses and some cobbles, but a living, beating heart. Tony Warren spawned it, H.V.K. nursed it and Cecil Bernstein loved it. And we, the actors, lived and breathed it. If I gave the *Street* nothing else, I gave it my heart.

Chapter Forty-One

They say when you are faced with death your whole life flashes before your eyes. Something of the sort happened to me when I left *Coronation Street*, but it was not *my* life that condensed into an incandescent streak but the life of the *Street* itself and the people who made it.

It is even sometimes hard for me to remember that events that took place for thirteen years did not really happen at all but were the figment of scriptwriters' imagination. Truth intrudes all too often. Elsie Tanner's television marriage happily became the real thing for me, but tragic real-life events have sometimes precipitated script changes, too. When my dear friend, Arthur Leslie, died in 1970, Jack Walker, the licensee of the Rovers, had to "die" too. In some television series it might be possible to re-cast a character, but not in *Coronation Street*. We all of us without exception, felt Arthur's death deeply. He was much loved. A quiet, kind, gentle man of whom one could truly say he had not an enemy in the world. We all missed him terribly. But life and the show must go on. For the cast of *Coronation Street* the two are inextricably mixed.

It doesn't seem like thirteen years since Elsie Tanner

moved into Number 11 Coronation Street with her daughter, Linda, and son, Dennis. Elsie wasn't so man mad in the early days; more concerned with her daughter's new baby and son Dennis's problems. Mr. Swindley was the draper, Florrie Lindley was in the corner shop and Jack and Annie Walker behind the bar of the Rovers Return. The Barlows, Ida and Frank, were much in evidence and their bright son Kenneth, just down from University and destined to be a schoolteacher.

In 1962 Ena Sharples, much more of an old dragon in those days than she is today, went into hospital with a serious illness. Viewers bombarded every hospital in the Manchester area with flowers and get-well telegrams. That year Ken Barlow married Albert Tatlock's niece, Valerie.

In 1963 my son, Dennis, back from an unsuccessful year in London trying to break into showbusiness, launched Brett Falcon, pop singer, on to an unsuspecting world. Falcon was less romantically known as Walter Potts, the *Street's* window cleaner. Brett Falcon's career was shortlived but the actor who played him, Chris Sandford, went on to become not only an actor but a successful pop singer in real life. Jerry Booth got married to Myra Dickinson and Sheila Birtles attempted suicide.

1964 was a dramatic year. Harry and Concepta Hewitt with Lucille and baby Christopher left for Ireland; Frank Barlow left for Cheshire after a win on "Ernie". Jerry and Myra Booth left. Martha Longhurst died of a heart attack in the Rovers. Tragedy for Mr. Swindley, too. Emily Nugent leaves him standing at the altar. The Ogden family move to Coronation Street.

Ken Barlow's brother, David, married the Ogden's daughter, Irma, in 1965. Mr. Swindley and Florrie Lindley left the Street. Ken's wife, Valerie, gave birth to twins.

The Street had its local elections in 1966. Annie Walker

and Len Fairclough fought each other for a seat on the council. Len won in a close finish. Ken Barlow had an affair with a local newspaper reporter and Ena Sharples was arrested for shoplifting. Minnie Caldwell's lodger, Jed Stone, is jailed.

Elsie Tanner got married in 1967 and Harry Hewitt was killed jacking up a car when he came over from Ireland for the wedding. Ena Sharples was injured when a train crashed on the viaduct at the end of the Street.

Elsie's son, Dennis, got married in 1968, to cockney Jenny Sutton and off they went to live in Bristol. The mission hall was demolished and Ena lost her home. Viewers wrote offering to put her up. "We know you would not be easy to live with," wrote one, "but we all have our faults. We will give you a welcome here." She moves into a new maisonette and Ken Barlow and Valerie take the flat above her. David, one of the Barlow brothers, decides to emigrate to Australia with his wife, Irma. Maggie Clegg came to the corner shop. Their marriage over, Steve Tanner returns to see Elsie and is found dead at the foot of a flight of stairs in their home. The coroner records an open verdict.

In 1969, Elsie is in court, accused of stealing two dresses from her employer. Elsie is worried sick but the case is dismissed through lack of evidence. Tragedy strikes the Street when, during an outing to the Lake District, the coach runs off the road and many of the party are injured, Minnie Caldwell and Ray Langton seriously. To the viewers' relief they recovered. The *Street* began transmitting in colour.

In 1970, David Barlow was "killed" in a road accident in Australia along with his baby son – and wife, Irma, came back to the Street to live. Elsie Tanner met and married Alan

Howard. Lucille Hewitt had her twenty-first birthday and a party for the whole Street in the Rovers.

Sad events in 1971 when Ken Barlow was offered a job in the West Indies. His wife, Valerie, was killed on the eve of his departure. Poor Jerry Booth, returning to the Street after a three-year absence, was charged with assault. On a happier note, Emily Nugent and Ernest Bishop got engaged.

In 1972 Ken Barlow gave up his house to newly-weds Emily and Ernest and moved in with Albert Tatlock. Elsie's old flame, Len Fairclough, began his affair with Rita and Norma Ford came to the corner shop. An insurance policy on Elsie's son, Dennis, matures and with the £300 she installed a pink bathroom suite at Number 11.

Alan Howard was drinking heavily in 1973 and came to blows with Elsie. Hilda Ogden threw a "society" party for her forty-ninth birthday and Alf Roberts and Annie Walker became Mayor and Mayoress of Weatherfield. The *Street* went to Woburn Abbey and met the Duke of Bedford.

The day to day events of Coronation Street are chronicled with loving care by the *Street's* own archivist, Eric Rosser of Handforth in Cheshire. Ever since the first episode went out in December, 1960, he has kept a detailed record, not only of everything that happened, but of everything that was ever mentioned. He knows, for instance, that Ena doesn't like eclairs. She said so in an early episode and should an unwary scriptwriter even so much as have her reaching for one, letters will pour in. Viewers are sticklers for accuracy. When Ken Barlow's wife, Valerie, hung out some dry washing, they wrote in by the score to complain. Ever since, the washing has been wet. One thing I can say is that the fish and chips are always real. As soon as the scenes are over the cast scoff them soon enough!

Eric Rosser knows that mistakes break the illusion and keeps carefully documented records, known as The Bible.

"Bring on the bible, luv," is a frequent call from producers to the secretary wishing to check whether Ena Sharples' husband died on Grand National day, 1937. He did. And it's all there, carefully indexed and cross-referenced in two black books. Eric Rosser, an ex-civil servant, began the "bible" as a hobby. Ten years after the first episode went out he submitted a script and that is how Harry Kershaw learned of his astonishing record. Mr. Rosser was not keen to sell his hobby so he came in as the official archivist and sits in on rehearsals and story conferences.

His knowledge is truly amazing. He knows everything from where the bus-stop is on Rosamund Street (next to Viaduct Street where the betting shop is) to the name of the amateur football team – Weatherfield Athletic. He even knows that Ena Sharples' Uncle Bill was a great yodeller who died before he could yodel at her wedding. He has a complete character dossier on the hundreds of actors who have appeared in the *Street* and another for the 20,000 characters who have been mentioned in passing.

Each character in *Coronation Street* has a biography, carefully compiled and stuck to in the script. Annie Walker, for instance, used to be Annie Beaumont before she married Jack Walker in 1937. Albert Tatlock attended school when each child paid twopence a week to go. Ena Sharples, Schofield that was, left school early to work in a cotton mill. Hilda Crabtree rescued a soldier slumped against a wall in 1943 during the blackout and married him six days later to become Mrs. Stanley Ogden. Len Fairclough was born in Liverpool during a firework display and, in 1943, joined the Navy for two years.

Here is Elsie Tanner's:

Born March 5th but refuses to say which year. Eldest of ten children. Left school at fourteen. Married Arnold Tanner at sixteen. Two children, Linda and Dennis. One grandchild, Paul. Divorced. Married again September, 1967 to Steve Tanner, American she had known during the war. Left for America, New Year, 1968 – returned home after six weeks. Widowed when Steve killed in an accident. Married Alan Howard, June, 1970. Has had a variety of jobs in Miami Modes, Gamma Garments, in club, in laundry, in salon, flower shop . . .

Has been model at local art college.

Interests: clothes, pools, once men but now Alan Howard in particular.

For me, the most poignant entry in Eric Prosser's "bible" is the one that reads: October, 1973. Elsie Howard (nee Tanner) left Coronation Street for a new job in Newcastle.

Chapter Forty-Two

I felt nervous and a little ill at ease when I arrived for my first rehearsal of *Subway in the Sky*. To make matters worse I was late. It was ridiculous but I was scared. The company, I think, were all expecting me to be a bit of a madame and my late arrival confirmed it. They probably thought I was going to do the big star bit.

Everyone was being very stiff and formal, including me. Donald Burton and Shaun Curry were my co-stars. I was rehearsing a scene with Shaun and the whole thing was going dismally. I wished desperately that I could think of something to set all of us at ease. Just then Shaun, eyes firmly fixed on script, flung out his arm in a dramatic gesture and thumped me heavily in one of Elsie Tanner's claims to fame. He went scarlet.

"That's right, Mr. Curry," I said icily, "do acclimatise yourself with the props."

Everyone fell about laughing and from that moment on we were all the best of friends. We went on to a highly successful and enjoyable tour.

When I came down to London to rehearse for *Subway in the Sky* Alan was still working on the *Street* so I took the train from Manchester. I shared my first-class compartment with a polite and pleasant middle-aged man, with a slight foreign accent, who smiled at me, and said hallo. I am used to people I have never seen before treating me like an old friend, so I smiled back. We started to chat. He told me he was a diamond merchant from Amsterdam in England on business. If I were ever in Amsterdam, he said, he would take much pleasure in showing me round. How sweet, I thought. He would be honoured, he said, to take me to dinner that night in London. I began to hedge at that.

"I'm terribly sorry," I said, "but I really am a very busy person."

Just then we drew into Euston. I gathered my bags and made off down the platform, the little man in my wake still suggesting dinner. Just at that moment on the opposite platform a train drew in. It was a football special from Liverpool. In seconds I was surrounded by cheering, jostling football fans, good-naturedly waving bits of paper under my nose, pleased to see what to them was a familiar face from the North.

"Whatya doin' in London, Elsie?" and "Nice to see you in the smoke," they called out.

The little man was pushed and pummelled in the crush. Finally I managed to free myself after ten minutes or so and a porter hurried off to get me a taxi. At my elbow my little foreign man appeared. A huge football rosette had adhered itself somehow to a buttonhole of his coat. He blinked owlishly up at me.

"You are famous perhaps?" he queried.

To go unrecognised *can* sometimes be an embarrassment and not a blessing. I was down in London working on an episode in which Elsie was to be knocked down by a car. After the bustle of the day's shooting I felt like getting away on my own so I booked myself a solitary seat to see the musical *Gypsy* with Angela Lansbury at the Piccadilly Theatre. I thoroughy enjoyed the show. I came out into a Piccadilly shiny with rain and not a taxi in sight. As I stood helplessly gazing up and down at the edge of the pavement I felt someone digging me. I turned round to see a very seedy little man in a raincoat. I moved away and he moved behind me. I stopped and he stopped. In desperation I crossed the road and entered the foyer of an hotel. My seedy little man would not be shaken off. Worse, he was muttering things at me. This sort of thing hadn't happened to me for years. I had no idea how to cope. I fled in a panic into the lounge. Suddenly I was surrounded by four laughing, very affluent looking gentlemen saying: "Can we get you a taxi, Miss Phoenix." They had recognised me, witnessed the pursuit of my ardent suitor and were falling about laughing. "You were on the girls' beat," they chorused.

"For your fun, you can get me a taxi," I told them. They did better than that. First they took me for a drink and then, like perfect gentlemen, drove me to my hotel.

We were in Bradford when the news came that the house had been broken into and my jewellery stolen. It was very upsetting, especially as I had no way of knowing exactly what had been stolen. I have a safe, but it is full of elastic bands. I could never accustom myself to going to a safe every morning when I got dressed to get out the rings I wanted to wear that day. Most of my jewellery lay around on the dressing table, lurked in the pockets of dressing gowns or was simply stuffed up the bathroom tap. There was no way of knowing exactly what had gone until I was able to go home and check myself.

My poor housekeeper, Kate, was in the house alone when the burglar broke in, and actually glimpsed his plimsolled feet disappearing through the bathroom window.

Mysteriously, the five dogs didn't even bark and we were all left with the uncomfortable feeling that it must have been someone they knew. I would like to think that the person who took the jewels had a starving wife and children, but the police suspect it was a lad who most likely threw the things in the river when the attendant publicity made them impossible to sell. Among the jewellery stolen were many things of sentimental value. The rings Alan had bought me and my mother's Victorian watch. It was a sad loss, not just in money as it turned out they were all under-insured, but most of the pieces held great sentimental value for me and were quite irreplaceable. One of the rings stolen was an opal. It was reported in the newspapers and, the next morning, Kate telephoned me at my hotel and said she had received a registered letter for me.

"What's in it, Kate," I asked.

She opened it and, very puzzled, said, "There's a bit of a funny black stone thing."

It was a black opal. The letter accompanying it was from a couple who had brought it back from Australia many years ago. They had sent it to me to compensate for my sad loss. How kind people can be. I have had the ring set and wear it, not only because it is beautiful, but to remind myself that people are worth more than diamonds.

Chapter Forty-Three

If I were Prime Minister for the day I would probably ruin the country's economy. First I would decree central heating free for every old age pensioner, then I would issue them all with mink coats on the National Health. Our old people believed in their country, suffered for it, fought two world wars for it. And for all that it is to our shame that most of them eke out what is left of their lives on poverty line pensions.

Maybe I feel this way because each day brings all of us nearer to becoming pensioners ourselves. Maybe because my mother is ever present in my mind. Maybe because that old quote is frequently circling round my small brain; the one that says that from the day we are born we are preparing to die. If I feel this responsibility towards them it is also because their love and loyalty has played such a part in my own success. It is often old ladies who walk so many miles because, "well I like her and I want to see her". I owe them – and I will never stop paying.

My heart goes out to old women I meet often looking half-starved of the cold in their thin cloth coats. I am very susceptible to cold myself and if I didn't have a fur coat I would probably spend the winter in bed with bronchitis. I used to covet a fur coat so much when I had holes in my shoes and I really enjoyed buying my first mink. I thought it was the cat's pyjamas. Now I value it for what it is; not a status symbol but the warmest, lightest coat you can buy. Apart from wearing mine to keep out the wind, I use it as a pillow on long car journeys, a bed-cover when I'm cold at night and, more often than not — a dressing gown.

Coronation Street scriptwriter Adele Rose and I had a habit of turning up at functions wearing exactly the same clothes although we are not at all alike physically. Once at an elegant charity benefit where all the ladies present were adazzle with diamonds and muffled in mink, Adele and I turned up in simple, unadorned white dresses. Aware the place would be awash with wealth we had both decided to play it cool. Adele gave me an understanding wink and whispered: "The nice thing about having a mink is not *having* to wear it."

She was so right. We should be so lucky!

I do love furs but contrarily I abhor the idea of killing animals to get them. I will buy mink because they are bred and farmed for the purpose, but that doesn't mean I am happy about it. I would never, never buy beaver, seal or leopard, nor should any other woman in her right mind. Tony Warren, *Coronation Street's* creator, could never resist teasing me because of my penchant for fur. As I swept into rehearsal, he would cry: "Here she comes. Catherine of all the bleedin' Russias."

I am fond of fur in more ways than one; warm, soft, snuffling bundles of it. My two pekes, Chips and Bossy Knickers, Happy Joe, the dachshund, and Blackie, who is not a dog at all, but a wolf. I got him from a zoo who had no room for him. He was only a puppy but at first, mindful of his origins, and unsure of his temper, we trod warily —

and it was not long before we found out he was as soft as the squares of bread and butter he likes to eat. The first night we had him we did as we were told and put him warm and dry in an outhouse. That lasted about three hours for, at about one o'clock in the morning, we heard something like the baying of the Hounds of the Baskervilles. The whole household rushed downstairs and outside in pandemonium. There he was — with a half-eaten window frame round his shoulders — the remains of his Colditz attempt, crying pathetically to join the rest of the household inside. He did. We bought him his own self-opening front door and now he comes and goes as he pleases.

Blackie is certainly capable of killing as any self-respecting hunter might for the chase or for food, but basically he is quite domesticated. Forbidding as his appearance might be to strangers meeting his muscled frame and sombre stare at the garden gate, Blackie is beautifully behaved. In fact he's a great big baby. Sometimes, at three o'clock in the morning, his baying howl brings us scurrying downstairs only to find he is crying with loneliness. We talk to him, I bury my face in his thick, dark fur and Alan will even tell him a bed-time story, which seems to do the trick. If he were a child you would say he had gone by-byes with his thumb in his mouth.

The trouble with Blackie is that he keeps bad company — my peke, Bossy Knickers. Blackie follows that bouncing cream plume of a tail straight into trouble.

"Oh, look, Blackie, chickens! Chickens!" she encourages, dashing backwards and forwards from the coop to Blackie. It is too much for him to resist. Pretty soon there is a knock at my door and we are in trouble. His last escapade was not very funny for the farmer but left us falling about with hysterical laughter. There was a knock on the front door and we opened it to face a justly irate farmer. "Now look 'ere, Miss Ponix," he mispronounced. " 'E's been at it again. Twenty-six of me best layers gone" (they are *always* best layers). He scratched his head.

"We'll say no more about it if you'll settle – but there's eighteen dead, two buried, two suffering from loss of memory and four in the canal think they is ducks." Alan, behind me, was pushing his knuckles into his mouth to stop the laughter – and I could only nod. We settled. Unfortunately we cannot claim income tax rebate for the price of Blackie's sins – otherwise we feel we would be rich today. And there is, of course, the cost of time, labour and building materials for the high walls we have to throw round our house to protect him.

He will never hurt a little dog but big dogs are another matter. Bossy has a habit of standing at the garden gate and haranguing passing canines, especially ladies like herself. She took a special dislike to an elegant Afghan Hound who regularly paraded past the house. At last she goaded placid Blackie into action. He leapt the fence and, baying furiously, pinned this poor shivering Afghan against the wall. Alan rushed to the rescue and Blackie got a well-deserved punch.

"You ungallant cad," cried Alan in sonorous tones. "Look at that beautiful golden lady. Just look at what you have done to her!"

Blackie began to howl miserably and slunk off, utterly ashamed of himself. Bossy Knickers, the wicked instigator, curled up in a cream heap on the stone step, seemingly oblivious of the drama, and went to sleep.

Blackie is used to taking orders from little dogs. Before Bossy Knickers he obeyed the late lamented and much-loved Mr. Smith. Smithie, as we called him, was a Corgi; cocky, courageous and one spectacular gentleman.

Smithie had a brother, Mr. Jones, who belonged to Edna

Walker, the head of *Coronation Street's* Wardrobe Department. Jonesie would often come to visit his brother Smithie at the Hayfield house and they were incredible to watch together. They never forgot each other no matter how long the period between visits. Jonesie would come into the room and Smithie would rise to meet him. Nose to nose they would exchange a polite "how do you do?" followed by growls and mutters of canine conversation.

Then they were off! Hurtling round the sitting room, through the doors, everything flying in their path in a mad ecstasy. Then, panting, they would sit looking at one another for a few minutes respite before the crazy round began again. Mr. Smith always saw Mr. Jones to his car at the end of the visit in a sort of "it's been so nice. Do call again" way.

Smithie was a character. Every Sunday morning he had a vendetta with the church bells. His last bark died away with the last peal. He never gave up the idea that he would one day out-bark the bells. He did not care for orders. Lying in a patch of sunshine on the porch and too near the car for my liking, I tried to get him to move. Impervious to cajoling and my raised voice, he finally deigned to move when I lifted my hand threateningly. He plodded stiffly down the hall and at every few steps cast dire backward looks over his shoulder at me. Bill and I were in hysterics. To this day I am adamant that Smithie tried to shape words in his growls – and some were even swear words. If told to do anything he did not want to do he would scowl at us over his shoulder and utter something that sounded remarkably like "bugger!" I swear it.

I was uncertain how he would take to Blackie. But little Smithie was not going to be intimidated by any wolf. To Blackie's immense surprise, Smithie took one look at him and bit him right on the nose. It was an unmistakable declaration. "This is my house and I am the boss." And from that moment on, he was. Between them they made the rules and kept to them. They staked out their territory in the living room and there was no crossing of the lines. A warning growl from Smithie told Blackie he was trespassing. When Smithie got out of line Blackie would rise majestically and warningly wolf-like. When we moved house to Disley my mother took Smithie first, and for a couple of weeks, he was once again king of the castle. Then we brought Blackie down. Smithie elected to show he was boss all over again. We waited behind the front door and as soon as Blackie padded through, "snap" – Smithie bit him right on the nose.

In spite of their feuding they were inseparable. They went everywhere together, the best of enemies. When Smithie died at the grand old age of eleven, Blackie lay disconsolate on his grave for days. Smithie had a grand send-off; a real wake. He had Corgi paralysis and we had to have him put to sleep. I insisted he must go at home with his friends around him and Ray White, our vet, came to the house to give him the injection. Poor old Smithie couldn't stand up any more and was in great pain. Ray explained to me that he would give Smithie a first injection to put him to sleep because the fatal injection would otherwise be painful.

"He will be asleep in half an hour," he promised and sat outside in the hall to spare Smithie the sight of his white coat. But Smithie wasn't going without a fight. It was three hours before he closed his eyes for the last time.

We all sat round on the floor – Alan and me, crying unashamedly, Chips, Bossy, Blackie and Happy Joe – with dog chocolates and coca cola and it was a farewell party. I don't think Smithie knew he was dying but for the three hours he lay there, none of the dogs left his side. We buried him in the American flag (we couldn't find a Union Jack) in the garden of The Navigation. When we moved, the stone above his grave came with us as a momento of that grand gentleman. It is inscribed: "Here lies Mr. Smith. The Corgi That Owned Pat Phoenix."

Happy Joe now has the honour of being the senior member of the family. He is eleven and having a bit of trouble with his back legs. He was hospitalised recently and put on a strict diet since he is much, much fatter than a dachshund has any right to be.

I have never met a dog I didn't like and I have never met anyone who didn't like Happy Joe – or Joe Joe as we call him. Since Smithie died he and Blackie have become great mates and Blackie missed him sorely while he was away. We were very worried about him for a time since he seemed so slow to recover, but then the two Pekes went to have their toenails trimmed. Kate, my housekeeper, hit on the bright idea of Bossy and Chips doing a bit of hospital visiting. As soon as Joe heard their barks he went delirious with joy and when they rushed in to see him he managed to struggle upon three legs for the first time since his illness.

To me, my dogs are my family. I have no children and, as far as I am concerned, my dogs are my kids. They are part of my life and I love them. They are so defenceless, totally loyal and they ask for nothing more than "good boy" and an occasional pat. And, unlike people, they *never* talk about you behind your back. Well, that is not strictly true of Bossy Knickers. She is a terrible tale teller. The moment I get home she bounds on my knee with the news of the day, snuffling in my ear and telling me *everything* Alan has been up to.

"She's a terrible liar," claims Alan.

Bossy is also a great harlot where men are concerned. The moment a man approaches she throws herself on her back, rolling her eyes. She never does it for a woman.

But when we all appeared on television together it was Chips who stole the show. As Vice President of the Animal Rescue League, I introduced an appeal programme from my home surrounded by my dogs. I sat in an armchair with the pekes and Happy Joe on my knee. Blackie walked in, looked disdainfully at the cameras and walked out again but the others were all ready for their moment of glory. The cameras started to turn and I began: "Many of you know me as an actress but not many of you know that I am Vice President of the Animal Rescue League and many of these animals are in need of help. My own animals, of course, need no such help . . ." At that moment Chips gave an almighty and noisy yawn, right on cue. We got loads of letters from viewers asking who was that dog that kept falling asleep. It seemed to me he was telling me I was very boring and did I have to tell everybody all that rubbish. Well, it might sound like rubbish to you, Chips, me lad, but it was a very genuine appeal for bundles of fluff much less fortunate than you. So go chew a bonio!

It is not the first time I have been upstaged by the Pekes and I am sure it won't be the last.

Chapter Forty-Four

No more television for at least a year, advised Bryan Drew, my manager. I was happy to take a break and let the Tanner image fade. But what to do? I could not sit at home twiddling my thumbs. Bill Kenwright, Gordon Clegg of the *Street*, for whom I had done *The Miracle Worker*, asked how Alan and I would like to do a little local tour, towns within commuting distance of home so we could get back at weekends. A play with a small cast, he suggested.

"What about *Gaslight*," said Alan. "We know it is as old as the year dot and everyone has done it but it is still a damn good play and there hasn't been a major revival in twenty years."

I did not like the idea of playing Bella Manningham, the frightened Victorian wife, a part light years away from Elsie Tanner but still, it was a good play. Alan would play my husband, the villain of the piece, and Norman Wooland, that fine Shakespearan actor, came in to play the policeman, Rough. To my delight we were able to get dear Diana Davies, from *Coronation Street*, to play the flirtatious maid. Cast was one thing – director another. Several were suggested but none seemed quite right. Finally Bill asked, "Would Alan do it?"

"Love to," was the reply, and the Browning family went into rehearsal.

Our opening was in Preston. The set and the props were sent from London. When we walked on stage and saw the set, we nearly fainted. The window, essential to the plot, was missing. The gas lights were upside down and didn't work, and the props consisted of such un-Victoriana as plastic butter dishes, flying ducks and a radiogram. There was not much time to the opening so we got to work ourselves. We went out scouting the shops for a Chesterfield, an aspidistra, even a carpet. (We finally borrowed one from the Preston Mayoral lounge which we were still using six weeks later.) The stage manager fixed the gas lights and all the girls got to work sewing curtain rings on to velvet curtains and bobbles round everything in sight. Diana joked: "Don't stand still, or Phoenix will sew a bobble on you."

It was very nearly true. Ten minutes to curtain up I was on stage with a paint brush and a pair of pliers. When the curtain went up and the audience applauded the set, I very nearly took a bow. I must say it looked lovely.

The tour was a sell-out smash wherever we went. Audiences loved the play and they seemed to love us, too. What began as a five-week little local tour, grew to over forty weeks and we played in places as far apart as Aberdeen and Bournemouth. I began to have nightmares about playing the part for fourteen years. It was nice to be back in the theatre again and to find so many of the stagehands remembered me. So many well remembered faces turned up at stage-doors to see me, people I hadn't seen in years In Bradford the old lady who made the veil for my wedding in the Cathedral came to see me and the

Pilkington family (no connection with my stepfather) with whom I had lodged twenty-seven years ago. Everywhere we went was a meeting with old friends.

On the tour of *Gaslight* there were many hilarious moments. I remember a night when Alan, Norman, friend Nell Hayward and myself, driving back after the show from Liverpool to Manchester decided we were too hungry to wait for supper. It was late There were few windows left with lights in them.

"Let's have some fish and chips," I said. "Great," they all agreed. "If only we can find a shop open."

"My turn to pay for the supper," said Norman

We spied a shop window still alight. Norman uncoiled his long lean frame from the car.

"I'll bring back everything," he said. "Pies, fish, chips, peas, everything."

Our mouths began to shape up at the thought. Five minutes later Norman appeared empty-handed, tears of laughter running down his cheeks.

"I asked for fish, chips, pie and peas four times," he said. "They said they could only wrap me up a taxi."

The lighted window was a taxi hire service and not a fish and chip shop. Norman had not stopped to look. He was, and still is, ragged unmercifully about the time he tried to buy fish and chips in a taxi shop.

The days ran into months and the months to almost a year. Our life was theatre, digs, travelling. It seemed to me I was back in the old days again, but I was working hard so I was happy. Our Citroen, faithful trusty steed that it was, at 70,000 miles on the clock was bulging at the seams with luggage and passengers.

"It seems ridiculous," said Alan, "to buy a bigger car. There are only two of us."

"You're wrong there," I told him. "We are really a family of seven on this tour and all their luggage." But for Norman with his own car we would have been eight. We settled for a spanking new Citroen Safari, capable of holding all of the seven and luggage besides. As marvellous as the old car was (and still is for all we know) we travelled a bit more comfortably and no one had to sit on anyone else's knee. And Alan stopped bawling me out for carrying too much luggage.

The tour went on so long that the winter weight costumes with which we started out became unbearably hot as the summer wore on. I had to get to the theatre earlier than the others each night in order to have my hair dressed in an elaborate Victorian chignon. Dennis Curry, my hairdresser in Manchester, arranged a network of hairdressers all over the country to come and fix it for me. They say a woman's best friend is her hairdresser and Dennis is certanly mine.

I missed my make-up girls, though. Any woman on television knows that she owes her face to the girls in the make-up room and I proffer my grateful thanks in the first place to lovely Scottish Lynn and in later years to Annie Whitelaw, a little Geordie lass, who fought off my wrinkles. As I sat before my dressing room mirror applying my own stage make-up I missed their friendly chatter as much as their skill.

I missed Diana Davies sorely when she left. She was contracted to appear in something else and had to leave us halfway through the tour.

Barbara Halliwell joined our company in her place. With Anna Gymer, one-time inhabitant of the *Street*, Alan and me and dear Norman, she completed our cast. We were admirably looked after by dear friend and super efficiency company manager, Jules Manheim, and Denise Newton, a fine stage manager and a very nice young lady.

We travelled on like gipsies from town to town until late autumn. It was sad packing the baskets for the last time, but exciting to wonder what might be round the next corner.

Chapter Forty-Five

The success of the tour kept us away from home more than we like. I am at my happiest at home with my husband and dogs around me. From the moment Alan and I first saw Sunny Place Cottage on the fringe of the Pennines, it charmed me. I should mention that our friends disrespectfully refer to it as "crackers cottage" but they probably mean its inhabitants rather than the place itself.

It is old; the date over the door is 1792. There is a stone-walled pocket-handkerchief garden, a wooden gate, a flagged path and a bare patch on the front lawn covering an old well that I once fell down. The cottage itself is three stories high with white shutters at the windows covered with an abundance of glowing virginia creeper.

The entrance, through a glassed porch, leads straight into a forty-two foot lounge. As you step through the front door you are confronted by a large wooden angel guarding the stairs, which might give a first impression of great sanctimony. A glance to the alcove on the left would soon correct this impression. A black illuminated demon's mask leers down from the wall. A step forward and you are faced with a low-beamed ceiling (a trap for the tall unwary), a stone fireplace, floor cushions, lamps, objets d'art, books, books and more books – and small bowls of water placed in strategic positions over the floor.

Entrance to this cottage can never be effected quietly. The visitor is greeted with flying, furry bodies and a variety of yaps and barks from the real owners of the cottage – my four dogs. The whole is presided over by my housekeeper, Kate, who lives in, aided and abetted by Kathy. My dogs would be a perpetual worry to me when I am away if it were not for Kath and Kate, affectionately known as Kitty. When engaging staff the first question I ask is: "Do you like dogs?"

The house is always a turmoil of comings and goings, of people popping in and out. My closest friends, like Cousin Ivy, Harry Shelton, Dougie Trevern and Nell Hayward are as much at home in Sunny Place as we are. Cousin Ivy comes and tells me I look a disgrace, expertly runs me up blouses and suits and complains because my weight keeps going up and down. Harry comes and looks after me like a mother, spends the day in the kitchen bustling round while Kate looks on (she even lets him boss *her*). Nell is the kind of friend who will give up her time while I am away on tour to come to the house and stay with the dogs while Kate takes a holiday. And Dougie, who always knows just the right words of comfort when I need them. Cousin Ivy is always popping in and out, and my dear friend, Diana Davies.

These are my dearest friends and my home is open to them. They have stood with me in the past, through the good times and the bad times and I hope they will always be there in the future.

Alan sits across the room from me now as I write, quietly fondling Blackie's ears. The small dogs are around my feet. From the kitchen comes the sound of warm laughter –

Kitty, Kath, Harry, Nell and Ivy. We are expecting Diana Davies, her husband and son for supper. The air is full of the comforting sounds of a home that is loved and lived in. Alan catches my eye.

"They want us to do a show in Australia," he says. "Sounds good. Could be a nice bit of bridge building for that series we want to do with Tony Warren."

Bridge building? I wonder.

Another bridge to build – another one to burn.